Thomas Brackmann

# I AM HERE TO FINISH!

Printed in Germany

Herstellung und Verlag: BoD – Books on Demand, Norderstedt

ISBN 978-3-7494-3046-8

# I AM HERE TO FINISH!

I love to travel the world.

Usually I only spend a couple of days in each place, but I like to live it to the maximum and try to do as much as possible.

Once you have seen a lot, and captured nice views of the landscape and scenery you can easily adapt to the local environment. It's always interesting to meet new people, be friendly, invite them for a beer, and listen to their views and experiences.

Luckily I discovered another hobby that you can easily combine with travelling and sight-seeing: Sport. Especially running, you can do it wherever you travel. Later I learned swimming, and also got a bike. So, quickly, I started participating in the infamous triathlon sport. Even as an average person with average stamina, but some craziness, passion, listening to advises and reading books you can get quickly good results.

For some years I have always tried to combine my travelling with running or doing a Triathlon. Wherever possible I swim, cycle and run the countries I visit. That gives a deeper meaning and touch to each place. Swimming in the currents and watching the colorful fishes in crystal clear water in Mauritius, climbing high peaks in the Swiss Alps, or running a marathon in the heat of the dessert of Saudi Arabia, gives a great feeling of self-satisfaction. You don't need to be a professional athlete to do these things, but if you are talented and ambitious, you can become one.

Now! I am also writing about my experiences. You might think! Oh, another book about triathlon? Really? Do we need it? Yes! The most triathlon stories are about maximum threshold, low carb diets, best training tips, train on empty stomach, keto diet, best swim techniques and so on. But what about partying? Drinking alcohol? Having fun? And more importantly, what about travelling and training in combination? Does this work? Oh, no! "Sorry I cannot go out tonight, I am training for an Ironman!" or Oh damn, I gained three kilograms again when I was on vacation. Too much drinking." Or the family issue: "If I do another Ironman my wife will divorce me". I heard that a lot. No excuses. With the right planning, spirit and positive attitude you can combine it all. Let's do this!

And why is it me? I might not be the Kona tri-athlete, or a Pulitzer Prize winner in writing, nor the most traveled person. But in that mix of all three, I should be rather unique: Double Ironman Finisher, 2 times book publisher, and traveler to more than 200 countries and territories, while working full time 40 hours a week. So I like to take my readers on my journey through my travels and races since I started doing Triathlons some years ago. I hope I can encourage people to do more sports, and don't take the triathlon as serious as it might be.

Therefore this book isn't a serious training hand book, or an advice on how to get the best nutrition, or whatever power meter to use. It is more an inspiration on how to combine endurance sports with fun. Train to the max, travel to the max, and party to the max. If you plan it all in style you will be able to finish Ironman triathlons in a descent time (12hrs or so) and go even further (Double or Triple Iron Distance), have fun seeing some of the country during the race, being able to party hard, and relax after a grueling competition. Train hard, race easy, and don't forget to smile at least for the finisher picture. Facebook and Instagram are waiting.

# LIST OF CONTENT

# FROM FAT MAN TO IRON MAN

"Triathlon is a sport for those that one sport is not hard enough", some people say. Others think: "Triathlon is a sport where you neither swim nor bike, nor run appropriately". The truth is maybe somewhere in between. But nearly for granted: This sport is for people with kind of midlife crisis or in their midlife period. Why? The most nonprofessionals or so called Age groupers are in their 30ies and 40ies. Usually happily divorced, or married again, got kids, the job is sorted, career is done or no career possible anymore. So these guys need to prove themselves. 40 is the new 20. In that age you realize: "Hey its half time. Now I can continue drinking and smoking and the story is over in in a couple of years, or I can make a cut". I can start over. Trend sport in these days is bodybuilding, calisthenics, yoga or Triathlon. All these sports are also good for posing in social media: Half naked of course to show the six-packs, biceps, and in triathlon the bike. It's bike porn time. Since you got the money to spend 5000 bucks for a nice ride and you aren't in your 20ies where you studied and any penny counted. You can afford. You deserve it. Period!

**Functional Vegetarian**
And so it started as well for me: Mid 30, overweight, happily divorced. It was time for a new beginning. Summer break done. I had 88 Kilogram. I was definitely too heavy. We need always a diet. That is business as usual. But now a new challenge has to be accepted.

Marathon Dubai in 5 months. Why not? Training books here, travelling there, half pro talks as well. Then training started. I did it in the past. So I can do it again. When starting it all, I had to change my complete nutrition. I became a functional vegetarian by trying not to buy meat proactively. I consumed only collateral meat such as chicken salad, when eating food on board of a plane or when I am in a weird country. Salad is no option, because of food poisoning. Functional vegetarian, what is that, and why? Is it because of the animals? No! No! No! Just because of me. Meat is bad for the metabolism, makes you feel heavier, plus especially red one supports creating inflammation. Downside: Veggie meals need to be bigger in size since low calories per size. Ok. Pizza, Pasta, Rice is also vegetarian food but in training always go low with the carbs because your body gets used to carb intake during the day and then on any race day you cannot fuel as much as you need. But instead trying to go with low carb diet and use the boost effect of carbs in Marathons, Ultras, or whatever. BAM! Losing weight is essential. Somewhere I read 1 kilogram body weight less saves you 1 % of the finishing time of a marathon. That's why. Easy! Piece of cake!

**No party is no solution**
What if you have been a party animal? And, you should start stopping drinking, eating crap, and having 8 hours for sleep – even at the weekend? What will happen too all the friends, the wingman socializing and the party peeps that names you will have forgotten after one

minute? They still remain on the dancefloor but you see them with different eyes - with clear eyes, since you are not drinking anymore. Now you are into sports. Alcohol has too much calories, carbs, is a cell gift and slows the recovery. Anyone telling different stories (1 glas per day is ok) is a liar and could be faster. No alcohol of course since it will slow down metabolism, is a cell poison, and has too many calories. Other effect: Slows down recovery. Ok. Positive: Calms you down. But the truth is: Everything in moderation and listen to your body.

**Shape up your life**
Another positive effect is when you lower the volume of partying you get better in shape and you see better shapes - especially in races. The opposite sexes and possible targets for coupling or training partners look fit and you can spot them with a clear mind – without dark light or increased beauty look by intoxications caused by alcohol. So dating as it should be. Good thing: When you mate with another triathlete you are not going on their nerves by talking about triathlon because the half of the time triathletes talk about their sport. The other half they talk about swimming, biking, running. That is a usual clichés. Kind of true since they can also talk non-stop about nutrition, race gear, race around the world, injuries, recovery, full program. Best is to be with a partner who likes to get up at silly times in the night, even at weekends for a long run. Only those guys can understand why doing all that shit. Yes, for a finisher medal where you rank only 1200 out of 2000 competitors after 13 hours racing in an Ironman. And

you are proud of yourself. In Olympia only the top 3 receive a medal. Yeah. No normal person would spend thousands of Dollars to travel around the world, suffer for half a day to finish average and be happy about such a medal. But we all are. Once during my first date with a non-triathlete she asked me: What's more important the bike or me. Guess what my answer was. Guess who is 'Single' very often.

**Lessons learnt: Live the dream!**
1. When you start with triathlon, start slowly and in moderation. Like in mastering any kind of topic in the world: Learn from the best to become the best. At least become better. Read, train, ask, and try. And find your best way of training and nutrition.
2. No excuses. When you travel, you train. Make it a habit. There is always a way to run at least.
3. By exercising regularly you boost your health, meet new people and you challenge yourself. Go for it!

# THE CHILI GHOST OF BHUTAN

They say happiness is the state's doctrine in Bhutan. It is mentioned in several tourist guide books or you can also find it in different articles. Before arrival I believed it to be more spiritual than Nepal, and more happily smiling people than in Thailand. In addition the photographs from the so called tiger nest, a monks house high up in the mountains promised very special moments of consciousness – being closer to God and endless happiness. I planned to visit this special spot during my 4 days journey to Bhutan. Of course: I had in my mind doing 1 arm pushup videos with the background of this culture highlight. Core training people would call it. I call it sight training.

**Hot, hot, hot: The food is on fire!**
The landscape of this tiny country was tremendous, a bit like Switzerland: High trees and mountains. Different artists would have liked to come here to bring these sights to paper. The people are very friendly, having usually a little smile on their faces. But the Thai people smile more – from German perspective, always complaining. They look a bit like Japanese. Additionally, I missed the spirituality and the overwhelming happiness. All marketing gags. Nevertheless I was positively surprised by the kitchen they have. Nearly every dish is made together with spicy chilly. All lovers of hot Indian or Mexican food will fall in love with Bhutan cuisine. Rice, meat, veggie – always hot, spicy with chili! Yummi! The food is on fire!

## Running up to the tiger nest

The highlight of this trip is the excursion to the tiger nest: 5 kilometers hiking up a hill. I asked my tour guide if I could run up and we just meet on the top. Luckily there was only 1 way up. So we wouldn't miss each other or better, I wouldn't get lost. Since I was in training for my first marathon in ten years I wanted to do some hill training. As I am not the greatest endurance performer that is still into travelling I tried to use every piece of opportunity to do some exercise. The guide was a bit surprised when I kicked off and left him behind. On top I got a great view above the valley. An unique experience. Light sunshine, 20 degrees Celsius! It was a perfect light and temperature. I decided to do a headstand with the tiger nest in background. After that I rushed through the building of the monks place. I took some pictures and inhaled the spirit, the thin air and some happiness as well.

## The heat of the guest family

Then we had to walk down. Next stop: Dinner with a local family. On arrival the family waited for me already with a so called 'Stone Bath'. After this little hill run it was a bombastic feeling sitting in the heat of the traditional bath. The bath tub was made out of wood. The water was at a decent temperature. At the end of the tube there was a mobile little wall with some holes. Behind this one the hosts put hot, really hot stones. These came directly from an open fire that was burning outside the house. The heat of the stones heated up the water. Since I was a bit tired but still having enough energy to read I enjoyed having a bath for around one hour. My tour guide took his bath right next to me but after nearly ten minutes he got bored, or it was too hot for him. The following dinner was like this: Chili with rice and meat. The kids of the house sang in the local language some songs for my entertainment. This reminded me of my home stay in a village in Kirgizstan where I also got a mini concert. Again, I thought for little money exploring strange, new worlds can be so easy and satisfying. The German writer Goethe once said a line like that: "Here I am. Here I am human. Here I can enjoy life" or something similar, he mentioned it in one of his writings. While a lot of other friends and colleagues I know usually spend their vacation in five star hotels I believed travelling in this way gives me at least a deeper approach to the countries and places I visit. Finally I found the happiness the people talk about when speaking about Bhutan!

**Lessons learnt: There is always a way**
1. Mental training is king. Positive vibes for sure. And smiling people in company make your day.
2. Travelling and keeping up the running spirit – nearly always possible. When 3 days in a country it is enough time to have a quickie: In Gym or nearby hotel or when guide at hand safe tracks possible. Go for it. No excuses!
3. Bhutan is great for hiking and trekking, as well for running. But the best is similar to Nepal: Finding the higher state of consciousness by the friendliness of the locals and meditation.

# ROOKIE MEETS ROCKETS IN RIYADH

Training: Check. Carbo Load: Check. Watch: Check! Race Gear: Check! Dubai Marathon let's go! Very excited. Already 3 visits to the toilet before leaving the hotel. On arrival again. And again. What's wrong here? The heat, the stomach, the mind? Too much water it was. Hydration is good, but too much is too much. Tried to implement all training and nutritional advice I had read before. So it came: After 2 kilometers I needed the first pit stop again. Of course no toilet available. Ha! What's that? I spotted ladies in the squat position right behind some bushes. Uh-oh! I believed the Religious Police or some referees will interfere. We are in Dubai not in Berlin! But then I thought hey let's do it. Same same. No problem. All good.

**Increasing intervals for stronger finish**
Then marathon, business as usual. Kept my estimated running pace, gels and bars in regular frequency, water as well from the aid stations. Felt like flying through the last 5 kilometers. Now I know what negative splits are. Great! Sub 4 hours as planned. Ok. My favorite training routine worked: Increasing intervals: 500 meters with 10 km/h followed by 500 meters with 12 km/h then fall back to 10.5km/h. Then up to 12.5km/h. I used to continue that procedure until I couldn't increase anymore, but falling back to 11km/h or 11.5km/h. The body and mind have got used to relaxing at a higher pace than the one I started with. Brilliant! So I could easily complete the Dubai Run. But now off to a festive brunch. Around 20

runners from Riyadh Road Runners club met in a fancy hotel at the beach for a celebration. Champagne brunch it is. 80 Dollars all you can eat and drink. For a Middle Eastern celebration, it's business as usual at weekends.

## Champagne brunch

"If you cannot run faster, go further", my table-neighbor at the brunch said. In the middle of the year she aims for a multistage race somewhere in South America. I believed she might be crazy. No advantage to that. That made no sense to me. Just the thought of that encouraged me to drink another glass of champagne. But here it comes; if you think other people's goals are too crazy – maybe they are just more ambitious? Surround yourself by people who shoot for the stars. If you fail, you still might reach the sky. Those people lift you up and you can achieve great things in life. Keep a safe distance from the people who drag you down.

## Above in the sky of Dubai

Aside from running and brunching, there are so many attractions in Dubai: Burj Khalifa, the world's tallest building. Great view above Dubai. If people want to go even higher they can go skydiving or bungee jumping! Even in January it's still hot enough  to swim. If temperatures are not cold enough at this time of year there's even an indoor skiing option: Ski Dubai! For mountain kids it's not fun of course, but for people from the flat areas, they may be pleasantly surprised.

**After the marathon it comes the next one**

In the past I never thought of running 2 marathons within 3 weeks. But once the running virus caught me, it carried me through and through. So the home Marathon race in Riyadh was calling. I could even remember a half professional 10 km runner who said to me some time ago, it's not healthy to run more than 2 or 3 marathons per year. But who listens to other people when you didn't ask for advice? Right! No one! And for Germans it is like that: They don't know everything... They know everything better. Still, I was worried of course. But hey he was only a 10 kilometer finisher. Never completed a marathon. What's the worst that will happen? I won't die. Just more pain. But as long you have pain you are still alive. Feeling pleasure and pain is all part of the journey of our existence. Isn't it? Yes it is!

**Locker room talk**

I finished Riyadh Marathon 5 minutes faster than 3 weeks before. Happy and I knew it, since it was very hot already. 35 degrees Celsius. I missed my PB by 3 minutes. And this PB was when I was 10 years younger at the Berlin marathon, a fast and cold run back then. Not now in the heat of the Saudi Arabian desert. After the hot run, off to shower. Normally not worth mentioning, but a chance meeting with JP makes it so. Old French running chap. 50+ years old. Old enough to be my dad. Strong finish in the harsh conditions of Riyadh with 3.17 hours. Top 5 or podium. Something like that. "How can you run that fast, you are not the youngest?" I wanted to know. "Hard training, and back to back, boy!" Indeed the next day he planned to run another 15k on tired, painful legs. I couldn't even imagine walking another meter. "That gives me the strength to go hard", he added. OMG! But he was faster than me, and among Riyadh's top running mates. "Grab the legs by the pain", Donald Trump would have said, maybe. I wanted to remember that for the future.

**Ice, ice baby**
Resting time now. At home legs in ice cold water to prevent the onset of inflammation. In Judo we would use ice spray on our sore muscles, in little hits. I read in some books the cooling effect directly afterwards should aid in recovery. In fact some months later, German soccer player Per Mertesacker said in an interview that he would lie in an ice box for consecutive days before the Quarter Final of the World Cup against France. It looks like I'm using the right strategy, same as the German players back in 2014 when they won the World Cup.

**Lesson learnt: Grab the legs by the pain (recommendations from French ultra-runner "JP"**
1. Increasing intervals in training helps to pull out a stronger finish. Better to pass people than to be overtaken. Better for morale.
2. First races (ever) or after a long break are the best. Great happiness and best results usually follow. A personal record almost a guarantee.

3. Dubai – rich in every aspect: Sports, culture, luxury, dining-in and partying-out.
4. Running back-to-back after a hard race. Recovery runs to keep going. Gives you the strength you need to succeed!
5. When cramping up, an unconventional method is taking a needle to loosen up the fatigued muscles. You have the choice, pain from cramps, or pain from a needle.
6. Having an ice cold bath or shower after a long, hard training session can boost the immune system, aid recovery, and help to relax those sore muscles.

# RUNNERS HIGH AT MARATHON BELGRADE

After some weeks of rest: Time for Abu Dhabi. Time for the Olympic Distance (OD) triathlon. I was joining only a team relay. Just the running part. Couldn't swim yet. And didn't have bike. Was still a normal runner, not a normal Triathlete yet. Running should be ok. Just 10 km. Oh well: When seeing all the nice athletes with their uniforms such as Supermen or Power rangers from all different brands: Sailfish, 2XU, Nike, etc. jealousy came up. Quickly it came to my mind: Can't be that difficult to learn swimming, and getting a bike. Triathlon could be done in future. No. Not in future. Now. Pull you strings together and go for it. So I did. 10 Kilometers running part ok. So far. No problem. But more jealous about the triathletes. I wanted it as well.

## Runners high is calling

Training for further runs went on and on after Abu Dhabi. I could do that shit all day. Highly motivated. Runners high here it is. Permanently. Every day weight loss in place. Getting leaner and leaner. Lighter and lighter. From 88 Kg down to less than 74. Yeah was a heavy chap. Interval training, hard runs, short races – all not that magical. By using running books for theoretical background made the runners life nearly perfect. Ok. Sounds nice like all other loosing body weight stories. But honestly: It is just going back into shape while being stupidly enjoying life in the wrong direction all the years before. And I like it!

**Balkan road trip with Marathon kick off**

Nevertheless the next trip ahead. Since lots of countries in Europe left to discover why not enter a marathon in one of the capitals? Taking 5 days off, flying to the Balkans, renting a car, doing Belgrade marathon first, then travelling to Romania, Macedonia, and Bulgaria in just some days? Why not? Of course with a friend – for entertainment, orientation and security. Safety first.

**No GPS watch is not a solution**

Kick off with the Belgrade Marathon. Marathon number 3 of the year. Aiming for another personal best. Faster and faster. Runners high definitely. Now I believed in it. As German planning applied, another best time in Belgrade marathon done. Even I had to ask other runners for the mileage while the race was ongoing. GPS function at my watch didn't work. So bad. So stupid. Now the rewarding beer. Then enjoying Balkan roads. We had already done Serbia and Macedonia and were currently in Romania. Suddenly my friend wanted to go to Moldova. That would be really close. In fact he was right but I didn't plan it before and the calculation wasn't that great for it since I was planning to ride everyday around five hours with the car and having enough time for sightseeing and party. But now he got also infected by collecting countries and finally we agreed on adjusting the travel plan to tick off Moldova as well. Nevertheless with our rental car we were not allowed to pass the border from Romania to Moldova. Taxi only. Walking also possible but not that great.

## Hitchhikers Guide through Galati

Therefore we quickly stopped a taxi at the border town of Galati / Galatz to get to the Moldavian country point. The taxi driver agreed to transport us through the border checkpoint just shortly after the border and then quickly return. Maybe just stopping for a toilet stop and a coffee. Country point is country point. We were already late and made this extra time just for the stamp in the passport. We drove around 30, 40 minutes through Galati to the border. Only then the driver recognized that he neither had his passport with him nor a permission to cross the border. Well, back to the roots. Another taxi driver. Another ride. The next one I directly asked if he had all necessary documents with him. I even let him to show the documents. So I had proper proof. Back since my army times sometimes you have to play stupid when you control people. I did not want to waste my time again going to border and again to return. Crossing the border was quite successful. Easy peasy. 10 minutes coffee break and then return. We still had a 5 hours' drive before us and to cover half of Romania from the east to the west to Bucharest.

## Delay, delay, delay

But the fast track through the border was closed. We had to line up. Three lines of cars waited a already for hours. It went very slowly. The check of cars and people took ages. After two hours a group of motorbikes passed by. They could easily pass the border. I already thought to go with him by paying them 20 dollars or. But in fact we didn't know exactly where we had parked our car on the other side. Only the taxi driver knew. Stupid us! Since my impatience came into the game i went directly to the border police officer and tried my luck. When he recognized that we are American and German he directly said we could come forward and easily pass. Hallelujah. The rest of the other people came from the former Eastern bloc and i guess they were properly checked since smuggling at this border crossing point seemed to be a good business. But we were just easy tourist on the hunt for another country point.

**Lessons learnt: Check equipment before the race**
1. For longer races better use a backup watch. Just in case your GPS watch is out of function or you forgot to charge it. Same counts for nutrition (extra bar / gel if race takes longer than expected)
2. Controlling everything (passport from Taxi drivers when crossing countries)
3. Plan flexible / spare tImes on tight travel itineraries especially when travelling with company. Anything is possible
4. When combining racing and travelling: Race first. Travelling second. After the race you can indulge normal food and proper drinks. And you can relax. Race is done. Medal is received. Check!

# BROKEN ELBOW BUT NOT BROKEN HEART

A biker is not a biker when he doesn't have at least one broken bone or a scar. Usually, people crash in races with other competitors, get hit by a car or slip on a wet surface. Sometimes, there are more stupid stories. I got a non-hero one ending up in the Emergency room just being back from that awesome Balkan trip. With lots of motivation, I jumped on the freshly bought bike. Now the triathlon treasure can come. I got a hybrid bike – a mix of a race bike and a city bike.

## With Christmas spirit onto the Bike

I haven't cycled since I was a teenager. I was so excited; like a little kid before first Christmas. Together with my triathlon friends Clemens and Jiri we were off to a closed Airport Road in the outskirts of Riyadh. He was the master blaster concerning cycling and triathlon. Sub 1 hour on 40 km Time Trials. Enough said. Typical conditions there were just 45 minutes away from home: 35 degrees Celsius at 6 o' clock at sunrise, 10 km one-way pretty flat, but open for heavy wind; no potholes, no cars. Nearly idealistic: "Ok. From time to time there are wild dogs alongside the road. Especially in early mornings," training buddy Clemens teased. "But then you got to be faster than them. Interval training initiated by dogs. Hell yeah!" he added. Oh well. Let's get started!

## Brackmann down, Brackmann down

2 loops done. Sweat all over. 2 liters of water finished. Dehydration? Learned a new word on that day. But hey: the first bike was outdone. Clemens and his friend waited at the starting point. I waved happily. Then off the bike and quickly to the car. OMG. I had forgotten my feet were in the cages. At this moment, I already lost balance and fell to the left side. Never mind, I am a black belt judo guy. What should happen? Just another fall to the side. Bam. Shit. Already down. The hands still on the handlebars. No proper fall. Elbow in a little pain. Easy peasy. Clemens tried to help me up. "Shall I help you? "No, I can manage!" When I was a kid we had the saying: "An Indian doesn't know pain." So, I also believed. But hey, I am a man. I can do it alone. Krgghh... Crack. The sound of my left arm. Tears of pain and back on the ground. The pain was horrendous. Then he needed to help me. "Shall I bring you home?" my friend asked when I couldn't handle my bike walking. I refused the offer to bring me home. I didn't want the guys to stop their training just because of the greenhorn biking guy like me.

## When you have pain, you are still alive

Stay strong. Each bump on the way home hurt like hell. In my flat I believed: Ice spray to cover and relax on the couch. That would help! Not! When I couldn't handle the pain anymore I was asking friends for help. Off to Hospital. On arrival in the Emergency room: A doctor from Lebanon. OMG! I thought they can only do parties in Beirut or find a mafia gang in Germany. But doctor?

Yeah, the Lebanese girls go to a doctor. I know. To plastic surgeons. But a surgeon fixing my broken elbow? Oh lord. Other people collect stamps as a hobby and get old. But sporty people? Dying on the way to glory, or break their bones and look stupidly ever after. Operation tomorrow! "The arm can remain stiff," the doctor said. Every word from the doctor was like a clap into my face. But with tears in my eyes, I thought: "Hey I can still run with it and Paralympics might be an option. Not so bad. "- In times of bad news, somehow strange ideas come to life. Hallelujah! So far 3 months off I calculated. No sports at all. For me, as a hyperactive man, it was the worst nightmare. Luckily my brain was still working; credit cards as well and with one arm I could still book future trips online.

**The operation done. The patient still alive.**
The operation was done. Physio started. Had to tap out when then physio guy tried to pull the arm further than I could to make it move again. OMG! I've never felt such pain. Even when I had to resist arm bars in Judo fights it was a piece of cake against this pain. To sum it up: 3 months of no training but eating more protein via fatty meat as some other friends with broken bones recommended. The healing process should be faster. I wanted to believe it since I wanted to race again. The Schwarzenegger in me said: "I will be back!" And so did I.

**Lessons learnt: Better save the arm than sorry for the pain**

1. When someone offers help – take it!
2. When accident – always hospital for checkup. It can be more harmful than you think!
3. Eating fat and meat for healing the broken bones. Skip the vegetarian diet.

# RUNNING THREE COUNTRIES IN 210 MINUTES

After the summer another Balkan trip ahead. This time, starting off with running a marathon at the beginning of the trip. Since approximately a year I improved my running skills by training more and more in Riyadh plus reading funny books from the German hobby athlete Achim Achilles or the so called White Kenyan. Slowly I developed the idea to run a marathon in at least half of the countries I visit. But ticking off countries would still be my number 1 priority. In September I aimed for my fastest marathon. As an average endurance person I thought 3.30 hours could be a good one. Once an old friend said: "Hey dude, marathon running starts only with sub 3.30". I never believed I could make it. But I tried to apply tips from co-runners, diet tips (less drinks, more fruits and lean meat). Becoming leaner and meaner. So I registered for a 3-Countries marathon in South Germany at the Bodensee. Start in the German town of Lindau. In between, Switzerland. Finish in Austrian town of Bregenz. Of course, I planned a quick visit in Liechtenstein to get this country ticked off as well

**Carbo load at Octoberfest: Prost!**
Arrival in Munich just before the marathon and there was the Octoberfest going on. A good chance to meet old and new friends. Just before a marathon where I wanted to get a personal best – not a good idea. But also at the biggest beer festival of the world you can do carbo loading and drink alcohol free beer or apple juice. Both are looking similar to the normal beer and are also

served in the big Maas stones. My party friends didn't really recognize any difference. Otherwise I would have to tell them why I am not drinking etc. bla bla. Nevertheless two hours of celebrating with them is enough since the logic and intelligence of intoxicated peeps is falling dramatically. Reason enough to head off to the marathon destination.

## 5 minutes coffee break without coffee in Liechtenstein

My hotel was in Bregenz the Austrian town where the Marathon finished. Since there was a bit time before checking in I got a taxi and told the driver: "Hey let us go to Liechtenstein. There we will drink a coffee and head directly back." For 100 Euro and a coffee for the driver I could get easily to the country of Liechtenstein. Cheap. Cheap. No bad deal. The driver thought in the first place that I am a rich guy that just wanted to bring some cash to the tiny country and save it from the tax hunters in Germany. But he was wrong. However on that day no café was opened for us. So had a just a 5 minutes talk in a little town just behind the border (thanks to Schengen no border security in place anymore). Having a deep breath and then back to Austria. Liechtenstein: Check! Mission accomplished!

## Race plan readiness

After registering for the marathon I visited the open lake side opera spot in Bregenz. The view of the lake in the background of the opera stage was stunning. Performances must be tremendous. However, having these dreams in my mind, focus on the race. I knew a colleague wanted to meet me after for  dinner. I asked him to wait at the 30 Kilometers marker with a can of Red bull to boost my strength for the last 10 Kilometers, to give me the wings I might need at that point of time. I was curious if he would make it.

**Personal best but Red Bull flew in too late**
Then: Race day. 18 degrees, light sunshine, Perfect running conditions. I placed myself behind the pacemaker of a 3.30 finishing time and could hold the pace. The lake was nearly the whole time on the right side but I didn't have really the landscape in my mind since I was listening to my body, felt it, and checked when to drink and to eat. I had a good run, sticked to the pacemaker and at the end just at kilometer 40 I heard someone shouting: "Bracki, Bracki here is your Red Bull". Ha! That was my colleague. That made me smile and pushed me more since it was a tight game to stay under 3.30. I could only shout back that we would meet at the  finish line. I didn't want to lose pace to get the drinks he brought for me. Yes! I did 3.28. Happy with the medal and the waiting colleague! Super! He picked me up with his Porsche. Nobles. Great! I invited him to a big Schnitzel and Beer high in a mountain restaurant with a great view over the landscape. A great day!

**Balkan country tick offs**
The race was just the kick start for the next days on the Balkans where I ticked off Montenegro with the stunning old towns of Kotor. Slovenia, with its capital Ljubljana

and again Albania with surprisingly lots of bunkers and castles spread in around the landscape of the mountains. Since I became now more and more a runner and triathlete somehow I wanted to combine travelling with this kind of sports. Racing at the beginning of the trips, and to get rewarded afterwards with drinks and food. Swim, bike, run, drink, and repeat.

**Lessons learnt: Party, race and travelling is best served in a mix!**

1. Octoberfest in Munich can be used also for carbo loading before Marathon races. Appel juice or non-alcoholic beer possible. Prost!
2. Special races such as 3-country marathon or swim crossing Istanbul and combining 2 continents are interesting. There are even expensive challenges where you can run 7 marathons in 7 days on all 7 continents (incl. Antarctica one). You only need 40.000 USD. In Istanbul they offer cross continent swim via passing the Bosporus.
3. The Balkan is best to be discovered by a road trip.

# FIRST SAUDI RACE THEN BAHRAINI PARTY

Then the urgent need for a triathlon. A triathlete is only a triathlete once he / she has finished minimum an Olympic Distance (1500 m swim, 40 km cycle, 10 km run), a triathlon buddy told. But here and there nothing going anywhere. The only one scheduled in home base Riyadh got canceled. God damn it. But luckily soon one race at the East coast of Saudi Arabia: Ras Tanourah. Serious training had to be kicked in. Getting up at 3 in the morning, up and away to Old airport road. 3-4 hours just before work. Just before the heat. Up and down the lonely track. When you get afraid of your own shadow its time to stop or to drink more water. There in the wild you are permanent on reconnaissance for dogs, cats, snakes, and whatever dangers of the desert. Every time coming in shorts and Bike shirts into the elevator sweaty like hell. Strange looks guaranteed. Always in my mind: I guess I cycled this morning more than you will ever do in this year. But everyone has different hobbies, priorities in life. Other peeps have 8 kids, can sing, or know all TV episodes from Games of Thrones.

**Race party weekend ahead**

Now the first triathlon. Olympic Distance at the east coast of Saudi Arabia. The last 3 countries marathon showed that I had become a decent runner. I slowly started with swimming and cycling in the months before. At least I could travel. Since I had good physio and orthopedic treatment I could recover quickly. But I was still not yet a triathlete since I didn't finish yet a triathlon of any distance. After personal best in the 3- countries Marathon I was highly motivated for Ras Tanourah. My first one. The first one you will never forget. Like the first kiss or the first love. Olympic Distance (1500 meters swim in the Arabic Gulf, 40 Kilometers cycling and 10 Kilometers of running). Due to proper planning I could arrange a Work-Sport-Party weekend out of it. Thursday business meeting in Dammam close to Ras Tanourah), Friday: Race and directly after crossing the border to neighboring Bahrain to have a rewarding party. Racing and partying. All planned with my French Triathlon friend Sylvain.

**Water of survival**

Race day: I was only afraid of the swim, as it was my first time ever in open water. Normally swim training takes place in a 25 meters swimming pool in Riyadh. I learnt freestyle just half a year ago. Excitement was on! Pushing myself to the next level and fighting against the water. Cycling would be ok. I only needed to avoid falling down. The run will be easy I believed. Out of all three sports that's my strength. Yallah here we go. The first shock after 200 meters! There are waves in the water, and no line on the bottom. OMG! "Will I die today?", I asked myself after swallowing a lot of salty water. The pool swim was so easy; even though I didn't like it, the water was flat like a table. And here there was another wave, Fuck me! Where are the safety boats? Safe guards? Baywatch? Anything? What shall I do? I tried it with breast strokes: Better orientation and less water in my mouth. I could outbalance the waves and breathe nearly normal. At the beginning, all new things in life are not easy. The swim had the so called Australian exit: After 750 meters out to the land, circling a flag pole and back in. I was so shocked that I stood still and considered just doing the half distance today. It would be also a triathlon but just the sprint distance. After nearly two minutes maybe I thought: "Today I don't want to die – but I have to go back in. If I want to continue with this sport I need to." If you go to hell then do it in style! I sprinted into the water and started swimming with a mixture of breast stroke and freestyle.

**Against the wall of Saudi heat**
Finally out of the water, my time was in line with my standards. I felt ok. Next, the bike! Since I was one of the last guys out of the water I could easily catch up and I passed people in front of me. That was a great motivation. In addition I trusted my strength on the run at the end. No crash. Great!  Now only running, get a finisher medal and t-shirt, pack up and then off to Bahrain to celebrate. But already after 2 kilometers I hit the wall. No energy. Weak. Totally exhausted. The 35 degrees heat, the sun, the humidity – all seemed to go wrong  on this run. The air burned in my lungs. I even had to walk. I felt so terrible. But my French race buddy had the same issues. Since he was more experienced and better skilled, he had small lead. At the end we were both done, but happy to have finished the distance. My first triathlon! Super. But now it was time to power up, bikes and gear into the car and heading to Bahrain.

## Indian struggle in Bahrain

We had to quickly go to Bahrain. Other expats and Saudi's had the same thought, like every weekend and the roads were busy. The time was tight because we needed to find our hotel, check in, shower, and off via Taxi to Radisson Blu hotel for champagne brunch. There, we aimed for the 50 US Dollar Champagne brunch. I already knew how awesome this drinking and eating event was. Only later I thought we should have stayed directly at Radisson Blu to save some time but now it was too late. But if you don't expect problems there will always be some to come. At the reception desk of the hotel the Indian service guy didn't want to let us check in our expensive bicycles. The 4 people suite that we booked would be too small. I tried the African bribery way with 20 US Dollars. No chance. Then I got more excited and a bit angry. I don't want to miss my brunch just because of one guy that doesn't have a clue about the values of the bikes (that we didn't want to leave behind in the car). I said at the end that in India 4 Billion people live on 20 Square meters and now here in Bahrain in our 4 people suite we cannot fit in 2 extra bikes? Cannot believe it! Ok. The comparison was not the best, it was a bit exaggerated, racist and not fair but sometimes such argumentation lines help. Apparently my bullshit talk didn't help. Now I pulled out the biggest killer: "Where is the manager?" Finally she arrived and we could convince her – I believe it was my friend who used his French-mon-amour-Cherie-charm to let us check in. Then: Hotel room, Shower, Dress up. Of course, we ordered a taxi at reception before going to shower. I think this time the German planning came into play. Now: Ready, steady, drink!

## Quick into the head makes you mad

As we had arranged beforehand two of our expat friends were already waiting for us at the restaurant. They had a lead of several glasses and plates and were already in a good mood. Even without their level of alcohol, they were happy to see us. Having fun with friends is always better than just partying alone. In any case, I planned to rapidly catch up with both of them. That seemed no problem since my French triathlon buddy and myself were still a bit dehydrated, didn't eat at all after the race and as a sports person you get "head kicked" much easier. Despite these facts, I tried the both handed drinking style. Right and left hand with champagne. Ex and hopp – rein in den Kopp – as we Germans say. Prost! In combination with some cold beer, great food our lamps went off quite quickly. For an after party we were not ready anymore and slept straight through from 9 until 7 in the morning. Bam! Alcohol in the blood but happy with the Triathlon finisher medal!

## Reward drinking after races

Even loving eating and drinking I tried to apply special diets without having alcohol and meat. I believed I had to compensate a lack of yearlong endurance training, experience and talent. Even after reading books and tips from other sports people having a more veggie diet would be healthy and productive for triathlon sport. Side effect: Looking lean, hot and being fast! Bam! Bam!

Bam! 1 Kilogram less means 1 percent speed increase. I read that somewhere. But to totally give up any kind of meat or drinks I couldn't do. So I started having reward eating and drinking after races. If I want to drink more and party more I needed to do more races and training. Easy! At the end it would be an average and moderation of training and nutrition. All balanced out in the long term.

Take away: You can finish a swim in any distance also with breast strokes, especially when orientation is bad, you are a beginner or choppy water forces you to.

## Lessons learnt: All you can race and all you can drink

1. Best eating, drinking party place are the bubbly brunches in Middle East. Sunshine, heat, and Indulgement guaranteed.
2. If you cannot run anymore – you still have 60% left (Henrik Olsson)
3. Checking temperature in your race is good, checking also the humidity is even better. It makes a big difference.

# BIKE PORN IN THE TRANSITION ZONE

After struggling in Ras Tanourah on the Saudi East Coast I competed in a Half Ironman Man Triathlon Distance in neighboring Dubai. The race would be a swim 1.9 Km, cycle 90km and run a half marathon of 21 km. Together with a Pilipino colleague we planned driving 12 hours by car from Riyadh to Dubai. The companion would be a verbal punching bag for me. Since I didn't want to ride all the way alone I needed someone to talk to plus in case of emergency I wouldn't be alone. Hey passing Saudi streets and deserts alone is is not the safest idea. Flying could have been an option. But I didn't want to transport my bike yet since in this stage my technical bike set up skills were as poor as my orientation skills.

## Bling bling bikes

After a short stopover in a random 1 star hotel at the border we headed towards Dubai passing camels, sand dunes, and more sand followed by the skyscrapers of Abu Dhabi, and its picturesque buildings full of glass and metal. Upon arrival in the race registration I was overwhelmed by the nice and very expensive bikes. There is a reason why people speak about bike porn at such races. People invest up to 10.000 Dollars to pimp their ride. Carbon, ultra-light, super gears, disc wheels, and, and, and.

**Triathlon sport against midlife crisis**

Every one shows what they got and what they want to spend for this sport. It looks like that this triathlon sport is made for middle aged guys in the midlife crisis somehow. If you are in your 30's or 40's you have already reached a status in business and family life and you look for new adventures and challenges. Plus you got the money to spend on it. Your life is in order somehow. You made your career already or gave up on doing it. People are married with kids, divorced, still single or whatever. You know already how to plan trainings and when to pull it out. When you have the passion for this sport you create time easily. If you are dedicated / committed there are no excuses. There is no bad weather conditions, no family or job is coming in your way. You just manage everything around your sport. Once I read the statement that Ironman Triathlon World champs are the most egoistic people on earth. In moderation this is also true for all the amateurs and age groupers but on a different scale.

**Tears on finish line**

The race went for me as planned. Since I improved a bit on my swimming and knowing what was ahead. Swimming went well. That was done in a bay. Flat water no waves. But as swimming for me is always a challenge, I was happy to be out of the water. For the bike, I held my horses to have enough power left for the running part. Even my Triathlon friend Wolle told me before I could smash the bike part since I am a strong runner. But I was too much afraid to have such a disaster like in my Olympic Distance event in Saudi Arabia. However I underestimated the sun. Burning like hell during the run part. Nevertheless I flew past nearly all the people in front of me. Great feeling. Terrific! With tears in my eyes I finished my first half Ironman. Check!

## Ladies night after the race

After some anxiety prior the race, there was total relief now. Of course I could have gone faster, but that's a typical sentence of a triathlete. But anyways! Now focus on the reward: food and drinks. Another champagne brunch in a Skybar of Dubai. Great view. Great experience. Nap time. Massage, and then for a dinner meeting with a friend from my study times. She had organized dancing and partying with some of her lady friends in the Music hall, a local dance theater. 1 man and 6 ladies. Best reward ceremony! Great. Dancing until 4 in the morning. Then back to the hotel, sleeping 4-5 hours, breakfast with another Dubai couple and then heading straight back home to Riyadh for a 12 hours ride. Stupid idea. Every hour 1 Red Bull or a coffee. It was not fun and this ride was more exhausting than the half ironman including dancing party after. Never again! However I survived the triathlon and the Saudi roads and finally arrived at home happily!

## Lessons learnt: Triathlon to fight midlife crisis
1. Triathlon is a sport where the people cannot do one sport in a right way.
2. Triathlon is a sport for those that one sport is not hard enough.

# IRONMAN IN THE MAKING

After the first triathlon races there was the need for a nice retreat. What better way to relax and cool down than on a cruise. The best: Caribbean cruises plus visiting some new countries. There are even cruises where you can run a marathon each day and see every day another island. Brilliant! So I travelled with a French friend to the Caribbean.

## Triathlon reward cruising in the Caribbean

In all my life I wondered how a cruise would be. All my ex-ladies, wives or whatever, they meant that we were too young for it. Every time, I made the compromise, but this time I planned this trip alone even booking a double room to save some money and believing some of my friends would join this incredible experience. I checked different cruise lines and routes but found the German boat liner AIDA cruise has the best offer concerning time, money and new country points for me. Flying to different island countries, such as St. Lucia, Grenada, Barbados, St. Vincent and the Grenadines, and others would be too expensive and is not that practical. In addition, I fell in love with this driving hotel with pools, gym, spa, night clubs, and restaurants and so on. And the best: Nearly every day in the morning waking up in a new country. The dream.

## Sunrise runs into the harbors

I used to run or bike early in the morning in the gym while the cruise liner was arriving at sunrise in different ports of the Caribbean. Dream. Sun is coming up. Out of the sea. The red dot gets bigger and bigger. Phenomenal. Side effect: Running on empty stomach. Should boost the metabolism. Wasn't hungry anyways. A quick daily 10 km run in the morning should work. Good alternative: Bike on stationary bike. Some core exercises as well. Anyways, I was happy to have some nice company, shared costs, and always nice photographs from me since I believed a woman as travel companion is always on photograph hunting mode. Even I had fun collecting new countries; it was a great experience to see the difference in landscape and vegetation of these places. There were national parks, dream beaches, volcanic islands and rain forests. All in the mix of the Caribbean. But the guests had a free choice. They could have also stayed onboard. But hey: if you land in a dream island why not discover it?

**South African wedding party**
Shortly after this amazing Caribbean cruise I headed off to South Africa for the wedding of my German-South African Travel buddy Christian. Rich protein load with dried meat biltong and typically South African BBQ and spending New Year's Eve in Cape Town and ticking off the country of Malawi further up North. However, the wedding should be great since my friend planned a 3 day bachelor party. BBQ plus Safari on day 1 – men only. Day 2 was focused on people from abroad in German-Bavarian-Octoberfest style (everyone dressed up in Dirndl or Lederhosen) and day 3, finally the wedding celebration. NYE at the waterfront in Cape

Town. Hallejullah! All the way Biltong: The dried meat from South Africa. Great protein treat after the races the weeks before.

## Endurance training in Malawi

After all the partying in South Africa Malawi was calling. 4 long days in this East African country. While I could book easily day tours on arrival (at previous trips to see and experience the country I couldn't do it this time). I stayed in a middle class hotel. Calling a travel agent? No way! Sim cards – No! Landline phone – No! This hotel was a big disappointment. I didn't even ask for Wi-Fi. Somehow I could only manage to get some day trips for outrageous prices. I could visit some boring paintings in caves or little national parks. In addition, I went to Lake Malawi. But a friend warned me not to bath in it, since it is full of bacteria. Therefore no bathing or open water swim at all. The only thing I tried to do was running through all the local people in downtown and having at least some mileage for my endurance training. With a bright red colored shirt and white face I believed I was the strangest thing they had ever seen. I didn't feel safe at all since I was a light spot in-between the poor looking crowd. If a white man comes to Africa he must have money. It's not racist it's a matter of fact. Therefore I changed every day my route, ran zigzag and made sure to be at the hotel before dark. Safety first. Trump would call it a shithole place. But every place has its beauty. Mostly that's the people. On my runs other locals joined me for nice talks about running and about how to get to Europe. Vodka and running connect people.

## Hamburger Hill Half Marathon

Coming back from Africa I brought the African speed with me. Personal best on a local half marathon. That was my goal. Yeah! I started again conservatively far in the back of the runners. I wanted to pass all the field. That gives killer power. Even having lack of training and some extra weight. Anyway. Mind over matter. At the end fastest half marathon on hard, flat concrete. Bam! Now off to Hamburger event I organized for friends. Around 50 hamburgers to be killed by just 20 people in an afternoon chill out feast. Collateral meat again. Yo bro! But soon in the evening: Pain. No pain no gain, they say. Shin Splint! A kind of inflammation for the shin muscle. No training for the next couple of weeks. Tapering pulled forward. Oh man.

## Malta Marathon trial

Some weeks later off to Malta. There I signed up the local marathon before. Again, I aimed for a new personal best time since it is a slightly downhill course, every 5 km equipped with a music band and stunning scenery. I became more and more aware that I can combine ticking off countries and run marathons or do triathlons worldwide. So I could embrace all the spirit of the countries in a much better way, meeting new local and international people for exchanging travel and race experiences and widen my horizon. Great. Travelling could be more intensive by this way. Either its swimming against the current, riding a bike up a hill or running on a sandy beach – there is always a country related challenge. And I wanted to experience them. Easiest way is to join a marathon run. For a triathlon you have to bring your own bike or you have to rent it. This time it should be the islands of Malta. Italian style with arabic background. Would be an interesting mix. But for this Malta trip my injury was still present. Bad luck! So I could only do some walking through the great capital Valetta. I felt like in Italy with all the nice buildings, Italian like dishes and drinks.

## Abu Dhabi Du

For summer 2015 I scheduled my first Ironman Triathlon race. Nearly all my social life and travelling was dominated by this upcoming challenge. After my little injury I had to catch up and do a race in another beautiful environment: Abu Dhabi again at the beginning of March. I knew this place from previous trips with Formula 1 race track, great bars and restaurants, nice beaches and mosques, and the team relay race the year before. It's just a great place for sightseeing, having a short break, and a doing a short triathlon. This time it was again an Olympic Distance (1.5 Km Swim, 40 km on the bike and 10 km run). I really hoped my cranky leg would hold up against all the punishments. Together with Triathlon friend Clemens we headed to the east of Saudi Arabia transporting our bicycles in a jeep. Hotel Check-in, Race registration, pre-race pizza, pasta party, and race...felt like a routine already. Descent time at the finish line despite of the leg injury before. Bam. Bam.

Bam. Now the after party with reward drinking could start. By chance I met another triathlon girl that I tried to conquer by chasing away another friend by saying: "Hey you got your girl at home. This one is mine". In fact that was the greatest take away from this trip: Having now a travel – triathlon companion with some benefits.

## Longest day training wedding party
Weeks later another challenge: 30 km training run in morning time, followed by being master of ceremony of a wedding party, and dating the new treasure girl from Abu Dhabi. All in one day. Redbull helped through the run and the day. Goodspeed later in the night and steel nerves as well since one of the bride made collapsed on the dance floor and my date had to do CPR. Party over after the emergency call from hospital confirmed bridesmaids passing. Shock! But for my all day performance it was not that bad. Next challenges could come.

## Dead Sea marathon
50 Kilometers running? Isn't a marathon not enough? No it is not. In 2015 I couldn't decide what I really want: Becoming an ultra-runner or better an Ironman? Why not both? And a 50 kilometers run could be a good training as well. So I believed I have to do it both. Overshooting is the key. Means swimming 4 km in a straight way, 200 km bike leg, and at least a marathon. For me it is always the mileage. Training by feeling. Former Kona champs did similar things. Best is: If you have fun what you are doing, you do it better than others

plus if you believe it's the best way for you then it is the best way for you. For your training partner or completion it might not work since he / she is not you. Easy. Get a goal. Get motivated and follow it. And for some people very important: Don't forget your Strava. If it is not on Strava, it did not happen. Bullshit. But we all go with it. We are doomed.

## Jumping jacks after finish

The 50 kilometers took place in Jordan from Capital Amman to the Dead Sea. Around 20 kilometers are slightly downhill. Also not everyone's taste. However around 70 people started in the dark of Amman. Every 5 kilometers water station. I just let it go when it went downhill. I had big respect. I believed when I do break or even push it will soak out my energy. So I just let it go. Since I was freshly in love again, I had to sing all the way. My singing is even worse than my running but on 50 kilometers stretch with just 70 people in early morning times, no one is listening. But me. And the inner me got motivated to run faster and longer. For each race it is good to have a punch line or a mantra or a visual that keeps you going, that keeps you pushing, that gets you through all the pain. The minimum phrase is: "Don't quit!". You can be taken out by race marshals but never give up. As the great Basketball player Michael Jordan said, if you quit once it can become a habit. So you might become a quitter every time when it's get harder. But not me. Not on that day in Jordan. At the end good time, places 12th. The Swedish guy in front of me made me even jump after finishing. That showed me I had still reserves left. Yeah left for the after party or for sightseeing in Wadi Rum, ancient city of Petra. But for sure swimming in high salty contend Dead sea. Happy to be an Ultra Runner now. Check!

## Seychelles honeymoon training camp

Together with my new triathlon friend there were common training sessions. Even though not that ambitious for an Ironman she was still engaged in swimming, biking and running. To have some synergetic training and travelling opportunity we went to the Seychelles to enjoy life. Since my impatience came into play she had one condition: "I only travel with you when you don't propose". Easy peasy. I just want to have training and fun in the sun. I was rather concerned about my harsh training regime and nutrition plan. Usually people get out of shape once they are dating. I strongly believed that too many drinks and Indulgement would harm my Ironman preparation. Or, just living from love and air? Never mind!, we might handle that in a proper way and any physical activity would burn calories. The Seychelles were not only great because of the red hot chili pepper girl, the islands offered lots of beaches for relaxing, running, swimming and sun bathing. Open water swims were a dream. On the small island of Prasline cars are forbidden so it was easy to use your bicycles to pull out some cycle mileage. In addition, there was the local annual carnival. Pure entertainment. Lots of colors! Great!

**Lessons learnt: If there is a will, there is a training (place)**

1. Sea cruises are for every age, also for couples, families, and singles. For sports peeps as well: Massages, Yoga, Bike excursions, swimming and running all possible.

2. Most injuries come from increasing power and volume too dramatically especially after big feast in Christmas time. Better increase in moderation.

3. When visiting Jordan you need to tick off ancient city of Petra, you should run the Wadi Rum Ultra Marathon, and at the end bathing in the Dead Sea for relaxation after.

# 3 WEEKS, 2 IRONMAN, 1 RITZ CARLTON

Finally it was here. Summer time! Two Ironman Triathlons coming up within 3 weeks of one-another, and a wedding to attend in Germany. In addition, some new countries to visit of course. Slovakia, followed by all the Latin American countries between Mexico and Panama. Average stayover – 1.5 days. Travelling by bus, plane, boat, and car. Bam! Bam! Bam! Ready to rumble. Kick off in Klagenfurt, Austria. First ever full blown Ironman race. So excited. Of course I could have trained more for the triathlons and been better prepared, but that's always the case. A typical excuse for a triathlete, but now's the time to focus! Training, check! Taping, Check! Carb-loading, check! Now getting ready, feeling the positive vibes, taking in the visual surroundings that the beautiful landscape can offer. In the army I recall phrases such as: "Learn to suffer without complaint", or "don't complain just fight." So I was going to push it all the way.

## Booking failure leads to glory

Still in my mind, the following thought: Ha! And why 2 Ironman's within 3 weeks? The answer; wrong booking made 1 year ago. So stupid! Aimed for Ironman Nice. But after the open water debacle in my first OD and the hilly forecasted course in France, better going for Switzerland, Zurich. But when it came to booking the flights the race organizers couldn't find my name. Goddamn. But I wanted to be an Ironman.. So I ended up with Klagenfurt and Zurich within 3 weeks of each other. The prize would be my pride, and a free Ritz Carlton Brunch invitation from race buddy Sylvain, since he didn't believe I could do it. So I needed to prove it to him, not just to myself.

**Nirvana making races possible**

I booked Klagenfurt via Nirvana Company. Nirvana is a Race/ Travel Company that buys entry slots and resells them together with a service package (hotel, transport, bike assembly, etc.). For me, this setup was heaven since the Klagenfurt race was sold out. Great! Buying-in via booking tour operator helps. Money talks and makes racing possible. In this Austrian case: Nice cozy hotel, a short distance from the race location, shuttle bus provided via Nirvana. All set. But come the morning of the race I was so nervous. I decided to hitchhike to the race, accompanied by a local half-pro triathlete. This Austrian man in his 60's, with calves like a 20 something, trains every week around 15 hours, and always finishes Klagenfurt sub 11 hours. With a big thank you I took the advice to consume a carb gel every 5 kilometers throughout the run, roughly 30 – 40 minutes. Later I came to understand its roughly the amount that specialists recommend as well. Learn from the best to become the best, and listen to the advice of your elders! But attention: Never try new things on race day. That can go wrong!

## Drinking the water of Lake Wortersee

The lake: Still, and beautiful. Overwhelmed by the atmosphere of the cheering crowd. Great! Breathtaking scenery around the swim start. Blue sky. Sun is up. So many starters. Warmup here, stretching there. And always a run to the toilet. I guess all the extra carbs I consumed in the days before the race; have somehow materialized on race morning! Not good. Finally the start. Never forget; push it baby, push it. That was the spirit. But at around 2 kilometers I started feeling cramps in my legs. Fuck me! Never had that pain. Don't want to drown here. What will happen after the swim? Still have bike and run to go! Mental strength came into play: Tried to meditate like I had once learned, to relax the cramped muscles! Only swimming with the arms. Legs were hanging as though I was paralyzed from the waist down. The last 700 meters were in a little canal. Right and left the audience screamed. That gave another push. Incredible! But now all swimmers merged and each one bumped into their neighbor. Not good! Every ditch caused another cramp. I hated it so much. I wanted to finish that shit! Again I was so happy to be out of the water. Time as planned!? Strangely I pulled out the time I wanted to have. Now onto the bike. Yo bro!

## Longest transition ever

People said that over a long distance you have all the time in the world during transitions. Take your time! Go to the toilet, get your material sorted, and make sure to eat, drink and re-fuel. Refresh sun screen, some might want to take a shower or redo their makeup even. Most important: Take a deep breath! So I planned. Off the neoprene. Heavy work! Cramping all the way down from my neck to my feet. I even fell over. Pure hassle! Took 10 minutes including the toilet stop!

## Sweets on the bike

Since I started as part of the last age group in the men's category, all the fittest ladies out-swam me. No surprise, I'm a lame duck in the water. This meant on the bike I had the nice, trained butts in front of me! Kept me going and made me faster as I was overtaking them. Sexism alert! Hey it's the other way around too. One of my female training partners once told me I look better in my race gear than in a normal outfit. Everything skin tight. So that was also the reason she liked drafting behind me for hours during training…? Ok. Maybe she was just conserving energy. In Klagenfurt I  overtook 4 different Catherine's in the first 90km, each from a different country, and each with the name spelled differently. Strange, the things you can remember after long, torturous bike ride. 1600 meter climb, 2 loops. Even on my TT bars I tried to climb up, because before the race I knew the following signs of weakness to avoid: using breast stroke during the swim, going out of the saddle when riding uphill, and walking during the run. Pushing at all times. Stupid maybe. Some people are even faster with breast stroke, and adjusting the cycle technique according to the environment can also be perfectly logical. The Ironman World Champion Jan Frodeno can also be seen to walk the marathon at the end. So, I'm thinking twice about it!

**After the race is before the vomiting**

On the run I tried to take gel every 5km, as the old man in the car recommended. But after two hours of the marathon I couldn't see them anymore. Bars and bananas were the key to my energy levels. Descent run. Even the last 5 kilometers nearly sprinting to clock under 12 hours in total. Missed it by 2 minutes. Happy and I know it. But the non-alcoholic beer afterwards didn't sit well. Nearly vomited. Medical staff didn't know what was wrong with me. Self-analytics: More salt intake next time. However, a tick in the box for finishing.

**Schnitzel protein reload in Vienna**

The next day was spent with Austrian friends in Vienna, schnitzel killing plus a quick boat ride down the Danube river to Bratislava. Slovakia as a country to be ticked off. In addition devouring a big platter of all different varieties of protein rich meat. Check! Return to Vienna, taking off to Berlin to Hotel Mama. Birthday Champagne Breakfast on 2nd July and celebrating the Ironman finish.

**Birthday – Wedding travelling in East Germany**

Then onto Dresden via train. The evening spent close to Semper Opera House, birthday dinner on me. 20 people, including me happy like hell! Pork shanks, Radeberger Beer and that great summer feeling. Next morning in a castle for a German – Lebanese Wedding celebration for Stephanie and Paul. Paul being one of my besties. Of course: Being responsible for a nice wedding speech for this great couple. They love each other, and love to marry each other. So they repeated the ceremony later on Lebanon, plus a Christian style celebration in Frauenkirche in Dresden. They even became famous, being show models for the Frauenkirche wedding magazine. Even made coverage on Middle Eastern TV for their bi-national love and travel escapades.

Another great week of planning and execution done. Check! Partying under control since only 2 weeks left to Ironman in Zurich. Had booked another big race. Hopefully the body will not be on strike and will be fully recovered. Challenge accepted. My motivation: The new finisher medal, and the bet against my French triathlon friend who offered the Ritz Carlton brunch in case I can finish 2 Ironman's within 3 weeks. Peng!

## Zurich for dessert

Zurich here we come! Recovery is relative. Nevertheless, fear applies. Asking Kona Kris for help. He recommended massages, protein, and amino acids for faster recovery. In addition I used the mental strength combination: craziness and rich food. Gained 2 kilograms. But never mind I will lose them again. Zurich Yallah! Rental car, hotel close to the airport for storage of the bike for onwards travelling. Got a clever deal: Nirvana shipped my bike from Ironman Austria to Ironman Zurich just for 200 USD. So I spared my nerves and my money by not lugging it around before and after the races. Splendid!

**No race gear is no solution**

This time I was not alone. A fellow triathlon girl from Riyadh also came along to race her 2$^{nd}$ or 3$^{rd}$ Ironman. Her bad luck: Race gear didn't come through. Luggage stuck somewhere. So she had to buy everything brand new. Another race rule just got smashed: Never race with new gear. Ha. But in moments of crisis you have to do what you have to do. At the Ironman exhibition we spent around 3 hours getting new tri-suits, socks, goggles, sun glasses, running shoes, and bike shoes – all the 'bells and whistles'. More than 1200 USD frittered away. She wasn't happy about it at all, since now she had everything twice. But at least she could start the following day. A race bike she could borrow. All gear issues sorted out. Check! So onto the carb-loading lunch. OMG! After lunch all her brand new equipment was gone. Lost or stolen? The shopping bags were not there! I have never seen someone cry so much, spontaneously. What bad luck. Maybe it is just not her race? First the luggage didn't arrive, now all the replacement gear had disappeared. We still believed in the positive side of life, and checked all the shopping tents we had been to before. And hey... lucky her. We had forgotten the bags at the sunglasses shop. So finally she could race the next day. She even smashed her personal best.

**Terminator pain**

And for me: Late afternoon before the race I also wasted some cash. Everyone has a race weekend habit, mine: Pizza carbs race day before. Followed by the cinema to relax and unwind. This time Terminator. 40 USD for Taxi to cinema. 40 USD Cinema and 40 USD back. Stupid? Yeah. But when you're nervous and excited you do stupid things. Never mind the cost. Some people undoubtedly think racing 2 Ironman within 3 weeks is stupid. However race day to come: Pain. Pain. Pain. Not yet recovered. But compensation by craziness, it numbs the pain.

## Legacy program to Kona

Swim start was a rolling one based on estimated swim finish time. That should make it smoother than start related to Age Group. While waiting among the slowest swimmers another guy told me to go to the World Championship, by the so called 'Legacy Program'. I could guess from his body shape and his slow expected swim time he would never be able to qualify through conventional channels. Same counts for me of course, to be fair. For the Legacy Program you need to finish more than 12 Ironman branded full distance triathlons to get into the lottery, and usually you're able to go! It's a kind of short-cut for average people with some extra cash, since you have to pay around 600 USD each time just to start an Ironman.

## Ironman Zurich to relax

I finished Zurich 90 minutes slower than Klagenfurt. But I was happy to have done it. Waiting for the Ritz Carlton brunch, but before that, I was off to Latin America to check out some nice countries on my list. First stop Cancun, Mexico . Hotel was a safe distance from the

American hotel 'castles' and directly next to a local restaurant. No need for the menu, I just called out "Burrito and Tequila, Muchacho", Now party time and ready for the celebration. March, march, another Tequila! From starting point in Cancun with my ironman body ready for the beaches in Mexico, a bit of sightseeing, dancing, more tequila. Off to Belize, the snorkeling and diving paradise. Snorkeling with sharks. Flight hopping through Guatemala, Honduras, Nicaragua and ending in Panama. While other backpackers need 2-3 months for this trip just 2 weeks would be enough for me. Limited vacation time and a country point is a country point. Focus on the highlights of each place. Sometimes it worked, sometimes not. Never mind. Mentally I was already planning the next tours. Off season! When back festive Ritz Carlton Hotel Brunch was waiting for me since I had now won the bet.

## Post Achievement Stress Disorder

Upon returning from this summer travel/race trip felt pride, but also a sense of emptiness inside. What do I do next? I gave this feeling a name: 'Post Achievement Stress Disorder'. I didn't train for weeks, since I had no clue what for. Ironman done. Even 2 in 3 weeks. But slowly the motivation came back since local races in Riyadh still went on. The season championship was still open. Fighting for first place and roughly getting the idea for the next 12 months: Getting faster! Getting stronger!

## Kill the dragon, win the princess

So I got my motivation back, I wanted to win the Riyadh Triathletes season trophy. Therefore, I needed to win every local Riyadh race against Majed. I always believed and had in my mind the big battles of Kona where the heroes fought each other, or duels at the Tour de France: Ulrich vs. Armstrong for example. So I joined the Duathlon. 5 km run, 40 bike and 5 km run. I knew I only had a chance if I ran like hell and didn't hold back. Lucky me: My triathlon girlfriend at that time was present. So I wanted to impress her. It's a centuries old tradition: The knight has to fight the dragon to win the heart of the princess. So I ran like hell. Always watching the dragon. He couldn't escape. I kept him in sight. On my ride could catch him. Flying passed. Now calculation in place: Is it enough to build the distance, for the final 5 kilometers run? Jumping off the bike with cramps in the calf, also in my thighs, plus half my core on the left side. Never mind. The victory was near. 3.5 minutes in the lead. I guess I would lose 2 minutes on the final 5 kilometer. Yes it worked. Reward: Victory for the day and kiss from the girl. All good. The winner takes it all.

## Double Duathlon death race

Weeks later the toughest race went on. 40 degrees Celsius. Double Duathlon. 5 k run, 10 k bike, 4 k run, 10 k bike, 3 k run 10 k bike 2 k run. So many transitions, so many changes. All these activities uphill then downhill, story short. One older athlete passed out, and then he tragically passed away. He was a 4x Ironman finisher. So sad since he was a good friend of mine, always open for sharing training advice. But in my crazy mind I had the following: I thought of the Ironman Race in Frankfurt 2016. One guy died during that race. People directly asked: "Has he finished before?" Yes he did. Dying on the field of glory with a finisher medal as an Ironman. Ironic, sarcastic. But dying in the moment of your great enjoyment when you conduct your hobby: That is not bad at all. There are T-shirts made like "If I die please stop my Garmin." Nevertheless in Riyadh each year this race has the name of this champ in remembrance and to honor his achievements. Heroes die. Legends live forever!

## Lessons learnt: Impress people for impressive results

1. Go out and find glory. Do it for others and do it for you. Good results are fine but better when you find someone who appreciates it: Whether it's a big audience, a small few, or just one loved ones; people like to be cheered on. Money as reward is simple but not the only motivator.

2. When sweating, take more salt. Gatorade, mineral drinks and electrolytes etc. . One guy died just before in IM Frankfurt, another in Riyadh. Give your body the best chance to perform, and protect it.

3. When triathlon race is sold out. Check for (triathlon) sport related tour companies where you can buy in. The prices are still decent. The service, excellent.

4. For faster recovery: A mix of massages, high protein diet , amino acids , ice bathes, Yoga, and mental relaxation all contribute positively.
5. When finishing a big goal like a marathon, Ironman or whatever it may be, keep in mind to set up another goal shortly after. Better to set up a new target otherwise you feel so empty afterwards, and struggle to stay in shape or to motivate yourself for anything. If you have reached the moon, make sure to aim for the stars after.

# THE WHISKEY HILL RACE IN MAURITIUS

Already at the beginning of my triathlon ambitions my French race buddy Sylvain gave me the hint to go for a triathlon on the charming island of Mauritius. Every year in November there is the Indian Ocean triathlon. Great landscape, swimming in clear water with the fishes, super family like ambience – and another new country point. Perfect. To have a good cost-benefit ratio I planned the combination with Madagascar. The flight is very expensive though. But in the mix with the island of lemurs, it would be more practical. Since we were staying only 3 ½ days in this paradise I had to convince my Scottish Triathlon partner to travel with me. Usually I figured out that country collectors and rapid travelers leave their wifes alone or travel though life as a single since the partner is usually the weakest link by moaning, wasting time for selfies, and money (better quality accommodation and dining out) etc. etc. But I strongly believe if people don't travel with me they will never go to these strange new worlds. However no one ever complained about the travel packages that I wrapped up. Or they are all just smart and polite?

**Drink the hill**
In Mauritius there is the whiskey label called "Chamarel". Different sub brands exist. There is a steep hill with the same name. As a triathlete you have the opportunity to climb it first in the race and after you can have a nice glass full of this yummy drink. Disadvantage for the local race is the strong current, the ugly beauty of

the water. At the end the beach run of 12 kilometers there was a little compensation payback for the tough water swim part at the beginning. At least there was the whiskey Indulgement for after party.

## Fisherman's unfriendly water

Rental bike pre ordered by phone. Saving the hassle of having bike cases in paradise. Just taking the TT bars and pedals. Quick fit on arrival; here we go. The distance for this beautiful but hard triathlon: 2 kilometer swim, 60 km cycle and 12 kilometer run. Sounds all good. But the swim with the strongest current I have ever faced. Mass start with around 200 triathlete enthusiasts and some professional guys from overseas. The water: Crystal clear, warm and soft, full of fishes with multi colors. On the down side: It took ages for these 2000 meters. Soon I started hating the little fishes in the water. I asked them: "How can you be so fast and swim easily why I struggle so much?" They didn't answer with words but with fast swims – the little bastards!

## Titanium legs beat the Ironman

Finally on the bike. 1 tick off. Survived the damn, but stunning water. With the road bike and TT bars it went ok. Little wind all the way through the landscape of Mauritius. Precious. Water left. Green hills right. But then the Chamarel climb came. OMG. Harder and harder it went. I even had to get off the bike since the ascent was too hard, and I was too afraid to fall off the bike again. Not another broken elbow and stupid off time. Better safe than sorry! I pushed the cycle up the hill. Felt so ashamed. "I will burn my Ironman shirts once back in Saudi", I shouted into the sky of Mauritius. Finally downhill and back on the bike to catch up. But in meantime lost too much precious time. Shortly before transition 2 passed a guy with an artificial leg. Bloody hell! Not only the gold fishes are faster than me even the disabled peeps. Well done old Titanium man! Beating an Ironman.

**Beach run not for fun**
Running home should be an easy one at last. But as well there was a trick with the beach. Beautiful white-yellow sand to run through looking at the beautiful water. In a vacation very unique. But in a race it's hard to enjoy the sight. Every step felt tough. Sinking into the sand is hard especially after the killer hill Chamarel.

**Wake up calls by lemurs on Madagascar**
Since I have been doing this triathlon endurance sport, first comes the hard painful work, followed by Indulgement of the beach life, adventures and reward partying. That makes the good balance of sports and party life. After three days in Mauritius we were off to Madagascar with a nice bottle of "Chamarel" in my hand luggage. A mix of adventure in the bush and at the beach was waiting. 3 days only. I had limited vacation time, like always. Expensive flights though. The highlight of the island is in the North. Diver's paradise Nosy Bee, Miss Scotland, my triathlon companion, wanted to see that point but we didn't have time of course. East was

the direction to follow. The road conditions were awful. TIA – This is Africa. Therefore we made a booking with a local travel agency offering us a mixture of summer sun, beach, and rumble in the jungle. Bamboos cottage after a long pick up ride from the airport in the capital was an obligation. Short sleep, due to hell of noise in the morning. A long high tone made us stand up in bed. Beside lots of mosquitoes and other little living things the noise was the killer in parallel to the humid heat. Finally we figured the noise was coming from these monkeys like animals – the lemurs. These little bastards were very naughty but sweet. The trial to smuggle them home failed of course. In a little park they were climbing on us and jumping there and back. Four, five of these ones were on top of us. Soft and cozy with big ears. Yeah!

## Beach massages with live cooking

Via Jeep we went further East, off to our beach bungalow. Overall the meals on Madagascar were really awful. Having eaten worldwide I could say the food so far in this place: Bad, bad, bad! Positive: Bungalow only 10 meters away from the beach. Soft sand and easy water. With camera and extra water in hand a 5 kilometers beach run ended in a half marathon. The sand was great, the beach flat, and whenever necessary running off into the waves. Swim-Run selfies followed. A great triathlon vacation so far. After training comes the massage with beach view and looking at teenage boys playing soccer in the sand. That's vacation. Of course having drinks all the way. But the best came in the evening by having a fresh fish, lobster locally cooked on a BBQ and perfectly served. Travel life is great!

Morning run: 5 km no. half marathon yes. Swim run. Super fun. Flat and furious!

**Overrated Mauritius but sweet lemurs**

To sum this trip up: Mauritius is overrated. The beaches are ok. Seychelles, Maldives, Thailand, Dubai are better concerning paradise and recreation feeling. But the "Chamarel Whiskey" is the nonplus ultra. Same counts for the sweet lemurs in Madagascar, the real highlight of this trip. And for racing in one of the above mentioned vacation destination the Laguna Phuket Triathlon is also a must. A bit more than Olympic Distance as well. The highlight: Swim 1.5 Kilometer in salt water followed by 500 meters in fresh water. Thailand landscape, nice peeps, May Thai drinks and Thai massages after the race – incredible! Bucket list slot granted.

**Lessons learnt: First the race then the Whiskey**

1. Rental bike for races in paradise ok. But don't expect perfect race or best time. For race travel combination with lots of stayovers in different places use rental road bikes and take TT bars with you in your luggage.
2. When choice between Mauritius and Seychelles go Seychelles. Better beaches, better water, better cuisine.
3. If you are travelling more than countries you can combine Mauritius with La Reunion and Mayotte – 2 oversea departments from France.

# CRASH! BOOM! BANG!

2015 – The year is ending. Should be like the whole Ironman year. With a race in a beautiful place: Els Nasos charity run in Barcelona on New Year's Eve. Suitable before New Year's Eve party in basement club "Opium". VIP style. But before this could take place: Lots of rapid travelling, X-mas celebrations, Gluhwein and more gifts:

**Travel ping pong in south west of Europe**
As mentioned before sometimes a world traveler has to go home for checking up on the family, telling travel stories, celebrating Xmas and of course combining the home flights with new countries. After five years in the sandpit for Xmas I planned to go home this time and be with the lovely people at the home front. The red flame had to join this great trip with an average stay of 2 days in each place. On the tight agenda were three cities in Germany followed by Barcelona, Andorra, and Morocco. Barcelona – Casablanca 80 Euros return. You would be an idiot if you don't take this deal. The Schedule: Riyadh – Germany (Berlin, Potsdam, Dresden, Jueterbog) – Spain (Barcelona) – Moroco (Casablanca, El Jadida) – Barcelona – Andorra – Barcelona – UK (London). Ten days should be enough. With will power, German planning and proper energy and money management – easy peasy. Ah yes: A New Year 's Eve 10 Kilometers run inclusive NYE party in Barcelona are a motivator.

## Ski and shopping stopover Andorra

Andorra is only a stone throw away from Barcelona. Andorra is a tiny country between France and Catalonia. Country point 2 hours away. 1 night is enough. People come here for skiing, drinking and shopping. Or country point collection. Nevertheless, we had a mix of everything. Riding on a snowmobile, dining in and drinking outside and stunning snow selfies for the social media community. In addition warming up in the city's thermal bath. Back to Barcelona the next day. Another night in this nice city followed by 2 nights stopover on the west coast of Morocco. Arrival in Casablanca and taxi marsh to El Jadidah. 5 stars resort was waiting with buggy rides, xmas food, massage treatment and beach runs. Country point included. Check! Last night of the year in Barcelona celebrating in a night club. Short sleep and off to airport. Visiting family and friends in London for a night including four hours for sightseeing, run-walk passing Big ben, the flyer, Thames river and all the other sights people know. The old year ended with: Fast travelling, sport and party – all in da mix.

## Meeting ultra-swimmer – sound of silence

Per conscience meeting with Ultra swimmer Juan from Barcelona. Over a beer he told how he trains: He is using a 25 meter pool for 20 kilometer open water race preparation. Such a little man. Does not boast or care about a six pack. But he swims with ease. "I love the silence in the water. No one bothers me there", he says. Usually swimming 5 hours in this little pool. Just focused on his technique. No head phone. Nothing. The water and him. Just the sound of water and breathing. Becoming one with the nature. I think he could have said like in Star Wars Rogue one: "I am one with the nature and the nature is with me." Floating and swimming for hours with this mantra.

## Record breaking

2016 should be a new record year. After a 12 hours Ironman finish time in Austria in 2015, by the time 2016 ended I wanted to be 1 hour faster. Every year getting faster by 1 hour will get me to Kona, Hawaii in 3 years. Dream big or go home! I wanted to have a new personal best time in another Ironman triathlon race: Ironman Frankfurt beginning of July. The first half year I completed different fast races in the Middle East and Africa (Senegal, Abu Dhabi, Riyadh). The times were promising. Got faster and faster - According to my standards. Another milestone should be the Half Ironman Triathlon in Busselton, west coast of Australia. The plan was to fly down to Australia and on the return to have a short stopover in Karachi to tick off Pakistan from my list. Quick n dirty.

## Sharks or no sharks in the swim

Busselton is just 2 hours south of Perth on the west coast of Australia. Like throughout the entire Australian coast sharks might be there. It definitely makes the swimming faster: Be aware of the sharks! For the bike: 2 loops light ascent but in an alley. On a rental bike with higher front post - no problem. On that day I could hold the bike pace also for a full distance. Best times seems feasible. Felt great. But toilet stop costs 2 min on the run. Finish around 5 hours– not that bad for me. New Personal Best. Could have been faster of course especially when I consider I was riding on a rented road bike.

## Quick into Karachi and quick out

However, travel wise, I combined this trip with a visit to. Just for one night in Karachi since I was a bit afraid due to the security situation. "Pakistan? Is it not too dangerous there?" my friends asked when I revealed my travel plans. I thought otherwise. That is why I chose to stay for only 1 night . Quick in, quick out. Hit and run. Sheraton airport pickup, gym time, hot bath, room service, night sleep and off to airport again. In fact I spent more time in the embassy of Pakistan for Visa application than I actually stayed in the country. I needed to go 4 times there. And every time I went I was told by a British-Pakistani: "Karachi, Karachi – that's the price of Pakistan paradise." But country point is country point and all the efforts needed to be done.

## Flip over as its best

One week after my personal best in Busselton: Motivation level is sky high. Shaving off by 1 hour could come in Frankfurt. Hallejullah! 2 months to go, to train, to diet. So my bike gang Majed, Mo, and Sylvain started early morning ride in rural Riyadh. No car, no dog, no human – the morning was ours. 40 km in the ride, up and down that gives power. There a typical hilly part of our 4 hours planned route. This time another side road.

Majed half right in front of me. 1 o'clock. Down the hill towards crossing road. No car in sight. Brilliant. Down onto the TT bars. Sssst. Power and speed up. Head down. What he can do I can do as well. "AAAAAAAAhh!!!" he screamed. I looked up. Half second later – a hole across the road. Off the TT bars, breaking, lifting the bars to jump. Too late. Whooooosh.....

## Jesus Tom and his fellowship

All I remember: I was on the back. Like a turtle. Shock. I opened my eyes. The morning sun blended me. I am still alive. Shall I move or not? What about the spine? Anyways! "Go for it", I thought! Fingers, Legs, Arms - all ok. Then recognition of dislocated right shoulder. Also one leg was bleeding. Pain in the back. But what about my bike? That was some meters away. We were around 40 km away from our parking spot with the cars. Remote area at the weekend. Walking, riding? OMG. Maybe when it would be in an Ironman race or Tour de France. But in this situation: No trophy was waiting. Why risking anything without clear status. We had to get a car somewhere for hospital ride. "Mo – please don't get me wrong. But I know Majed longer than you he will come with me to hospital". Someone Arabic speaking should take care for the damaged rider. Later I realized 2 years ago on the same weekend I fell off my other bike.

## Tears and screams

However in hospital I was surrounded by some of my favorite people of both my triathlon and social life. I felt like Jesus and his followers. I waited for the announcement: surgery on the next day. Frankfurt Ironman still in my mind. When the doctor came he didn't make any big intention to go ahead quickly. First everything must be healed. Kind of. Next week. Shit. Will lose another week. I could be lucky that nothing more happened. Yeah baby. Doing that shit not for money just for fun. And I am still an average finisher. Tears again. Mama. But the tears wiped away when the nurse put antiseptic on bloody back. Scream! Fuck me! It felt like the back is burning. Hell!

## Post traumatic bike disorder

Ever since I will not forget this kind of pain. Ever since I don't train hills anymore. Mentally damaged for life I guess. Pro Athlete Lionel Sanders had similar experience: Usually he only trains indoors. Better safe than sorry. In addition: It can be more efficient to use your turbo trainer or Gym bike for cycling: You can work on emails, watch TV, listening to radio, safe time going to special bike tracks and and and. Downside: You might not know how to handle your bike in reality. Best is to do everything in moderation. However for me after that crash all I was thinking of was to recover as fast as possible.

## Handicap birthday party in Frankfurt

No sports for three months though. All I had planned: First Ironman Triathlon in Frankfurt, Germany at 3$^{rd}$ July including birthday party and then off to pacific island hopping with lean body for great Facebook pictures and attracting peeps. But due to the accident I was the one arm bandito with a sling. Race: No! - Birthday party and travelling: Yes!

## Kids cuddling in Helsinki

I didn't want to see other people racing in Frankfurt since I couldn't participate; I booked a night flight to Helsinki on my birthday. Ok, 15 hours stay for around 400 Euros is a bit expensive. But visiting friends and my own god daughters, any price should be alright. Plus I calculated free accommodation, food, drinks and fun. That would balance all the other costs. And again Germany was playing soccer against Italy. European Championship Quarter finals. When departing it was 0:0 Germany – Italy. On arrival 2 stewardesses and 5 remaining guests grouped around a little smart phone to follow the penalty shootout. All other guests had left the plane already. But the Germans were keen to suffer until the end. All the top stars like Schweinsteiger failed but the newbies in the German team made sure to have finally a success against the Italians in a big tournament. A perfect birthday present for me. Thank you very much indeed! Then, quickly off to Nauru, Marshall Islands, and Kiribati. Broken wings make a better swimmer thanks to the pull boy. Tick tick tick. Islands around in the pacific. Touché.

**Lessons learnt: Barcelona for Tapas, triathlon and party fun**

1. New Year's Eve Party Run is possible in Barcelona
2. Busselton Ironman 70.3. Pretty flat, pretty fast, pretty sharky.
3. Busselton (Western Australia, Perth region) is surrounded by wineries and little breweries. Great to explore after triathlons.
4. Rental bike for Ironman races are fully ok.
5. Busselton (comfort first, aero second! / rental is ok)

# DAY OF THUNDERAT IRONMAN MALLORCA

If you want to combine a nice challenging Ironman Triathlon Race with the spirit of vacation, but still having the being home feeling – then Ironman Mallorca is the best option for an average Riyadh Triathlete expat. Nearly 80 percent of all participants in Mallorca are either British or German. No wonder the island of Mallorca is a favorite touristic spot for both: Germans and British for their summer holidays. In 2016 Ironman Mallorca took place for the 3rd time on 24th of September. For me it was perfect because we had a long weekend due to Saudi National Day.

## Frankfurt Fail

It should have been my 2nd Ironman Race in 2016 after Frankfurt in July. But after that terrible accident I had to cancel my planned personal best time in Frankfurt and I wasn't sure if I can get even recovered from my collar bone injury until Ironman Mallorca. Despite of having a break of any kind of sport activity in June and July, I believed my body would heal and I could catch up with all training that I assumed to have in for having a descent finish. From previous Ironman races I knew how to get quickly back into shape, balancing the progress to prevent injury but also keeping an eye on the healing bone.

**Train with the best to become the best**

Knowing there will be an open water ocean swim and considering swim to be my worst discipline plus constraints because of my damaged shoulder I tried to put more effort in swim preparation. I ended up with a weekly mileage of around 8 Km in the pool. The longest shot was for about 5 kilometers. Similarly I did my training with the bike. Mallorca is quite hilly and has an ascent of about 1500m in total. Therefore I trained in hilly conditions and made as well long shots with a day mileage of up to 200 km. Weekly mileage for 3 weeks in a row: 300 km. Plus I trained with our best bikers in town: Irish Powerman Gareth Gallagher, Swedish Kona hope Kris, 3 x Ironman Finisher Katharina, and Wheelers Chairman Clemens. So I could steal some tips and mental support. For Running I didn't put that much effort in. I had max only 60-70 km on the weekly clock. The muscles and the limited time were the constraint here. In total I focused on long shots. No sprints, no intervals, pure mileage here. Even with Saudi running hero Majed I had only a coffee for psychologic preparation. So I felt ready for my third Ironman. I knew: When I enter the water I will finish the race and get the medal. I aimed to finish in around 14 hours considering all constraints that I faced up to the race.

**5 minutes bike fitting**

I arrived 2 nights before the race at Palma Airport and I had pre-arranged a personal driver that should bring me to a bike rental place (Palma on bike). There I ordered a Carbon race bike since Riyadh Airport still were not able to transport my bike, a shipping were too complicated and anyways I wanted to return via Algiers (Algeria) to get a new country point ticked off. So I thought overall racing an Ironman on a descent Road bike should be ok. I made the fitting just as a quick 5 minutes job (saddle height, breaks, and gears) and fixed extra TT Handle bars. So it was sorted. My hostel was only 500 meters away from the Expo Area so I could walk to Start, Finish, and registration. Basically that's the good thing in Mallorca that a lot of accommodations are close to the race area. Furthermore lots of them have a connected restaurant in pedestrian area with sea / harbor view. Perfect for the after race party / drink.

## The day before – Pizza-wine power

The day before the race is business as usual: Easy peasy swim together with Triathlon buddy Wolle Kuhl from Germany in the clear water of the lagoon of Alcudia. Surprisingly I had a great swim. No pain. We tried both: Swimming with and without wetsuit. Afterwards I had my traditional Pizza-before-the-Race for lunch plus a glas of red wine. Per coincidence I had a glas of red wine before Ironman 70.3 Bahrain 2015 and Ironman 70.3 Busselton in Australia 2016. Both times I had fast races the following day and was very happy about my overall result. So I believed in the power of pizza and wine. Never change a running system. Strangely in the evening before the race management announced no wetsuit competition. Usually the announcement takes place on race morning

1 hour before the start. Nevertheless I was prepared for all. Early bed time, lots of water, and alarm clock set for 5 am. Excitement? Yes. Ok. A bit. Nothing major. Not like before other races. I didn't expect a personal best this time – too many limiting factors were in place. But I also knew I will finish. Period! The question was only in what condition I will manage passing the finish line. Lack of training, training in a rush and still not yet 100% recovered. But at least the mind was fresh and ready for action.

## Ready steady go and swim

I had the best sleep ever before any triathlon: Deep and long. I was quite relaxed. I knew what's coming now: Preparation of Bike with bottles and final check of transition bags with running shoes, gels, sun glasses etc. Then the surprise: Wetsuit allowed. For me, as an injured bad swimmer it was great. So: Quickly back to hotel and getting ready. Wetsuit on, warming up, stretching, waiting. Finally the start. It was in waves. Bad swimmers start at the end of the field. The top crowd at beginning. That should reduce anxiety for beginners and makes it smoother. It was straight 1.2 km out and turn towards the land again and having an Australian Exit at km 2.4. Meaning: You have to run out of the water and run into the water again. Luckily I didn't have any pain and could do my steady pace. Typically I lose the direction but this time it was quite ok. Extra turns as usual. I didn't get cramps like in my previous ironman races. So I could swim without any interruption. I ended up with 1.36 hour. In the field it was still a bad time. But for me only 6 minutes slower than my best time. Surprise. That gave me encouragement for the bike.

## Bike – Raining Ironman

My plan was to have an average pace of 30 Kilometers / hour during the bumpy and hilly roads on the first half to save energy for the big hill at km 105. It has an ascent for around 10 kilometers and a curvy downhill. After up and down at 120 Kilometers I planned to speed up and to see how much reserves I still have left since I couldn't really train hill training before and was still a bit afraid of going downhill. Even riding on this road bike and not my own TT Baby I made good progress and everything was according to plan (Drinking every 10km, a Carbo gel every 20km, taking minerals at each aid station etc.). I passed all people in front of me because my swim time was that bad. Then I entered the hill and was surprise about the climb. It was ok. So my training was enough apparently. But I also saw the shadowy clouds coming up and suddenly it went dark.

## Too much rain over paradise

A thunderstorm came over us with heavy rain. I was not looking forward to the downhill if the rain sustained. Luckily when I reached the top the rain stopped. All people I passed uphill got me when it went down. I was so afraid of falling again, also having a bike that I am not used to. However the curves were really narrow. I saw behind the little walls of the curves. It went straight down

400-500 meters. If you don't get the curve, you will get the dead. For sure. The pace went down to 5 Kilometers per hour. That was my average speed sometimes. I hoped to speed up between 120 and 180 km to clock sub 6 hours. But reaching the valley the rain started again. I was meanwhile 45 minutes behind schedule. Wet all over. The socks, shoes – all drained by water. Luckily it wasn't that cold. But the rain and the water on the streets cost an average pace of 4 – 6 km / hour. The roads made people fall since it was very slippery. Meanwhile the sight was just about 30 meters. So I had to slow down again. At the end of the 180 km I still felt fresh. 6.27 Hours.

**Daylight finish vs Night owl runner**

Somehow I dreamed to make personal best still (sub 12). After biking I had only 8.10 hours. If I could run far below 4 hours then I could make it. Even feeling not that well prepared for the final Marathon – the temperature was just around 20 something degrees and the rain stopped in the meantime. So I started off quite nice. Unluckily my watch didn't show me any pace anymore. Maybe it is not water proof anymore, or the battery died. However I couldn't control my pace. Stupidly I had to ask other people about the pace they have to get a kind of clue about mine. Somehow I got tired and didn't have my pacemaker watch with me so I made a just- run- through- Marathon out of it. But also being happy that I reached this far. At the end I could finish in 4.12 having 10 kilometers an hour. With a proper watch could have made maybe sub 4 hours. End result 12.29. Personal best times in transition. Aside of no injuries and shoulder pain free after the race – a positive result.

## After an Ironman is before an Ironman
After having some days of break I started preparation for Challenge Wanaka in February 2017: More speed work, more intervals. I believe I can make it in below 12 hours even it's a hard race since the water is choppy, hilly bike leg and the marathon is more a trail run. But people say the landscape and views are stunning. That could balance out the harsh conditions.

## Lessons learnt: Mallorca - The Mecca of cyclists
1. After parties granted on Mallorca. All the carbs you burned in the race will be picked up easily after.
2. Accommodations can be found closely to the start and finish. In the morning you can walk to your race.
3. Mallorca is a good place for combining vacation and training especially for cycling since a lot of bike rental companies are available.

# THE FAR SIDE OF THE WORLD

In February 2017 another great trip including another Iron distance race. Normally I do an Ironman first in a trip followed by country hopping. Then all delivery is done and eating and drinking can take place as relaxation and rewarding. But on this trip wedding first in New Zealand in Wanaka and nearly 3 weeks later same place Challenge Wanaka for a race. In between to cover Cook Islands, Solomon Islands - all in Pacific. All dream destinations – not only for honeymooners.

## Wedding party at the most beautiful lake in the world

First to the wedding of a friend. For 2 years I was begging the groom to set up the right date for the wedding party around my Challenge Wanaka. He tried his best but wedding location was always booked. So bad. It should be a typical Kiwi wedding. Best at the lake of Wanaka. It is one of the most beautiful lakes in the world encircle by hills and mountains. Even in summer time you can spot layers of snow on the peaks. The wedding place: Hotel Edgewater close to the lake. The guests have a tremendous view to the water and can chill at cozy temperatures and enjoy tapas and nice drinks. Even after the indulging dinner in the evening the lake invites the guests for relaxing and listing to the music. The light of the stars dancing on the surface of the water together with the party vibe: unforgettable.

## Pre testing the upcoming race

We will see in 2 weeks. But now pre-holidays and some last training. Nevertheless I ran around Lake Wanaka as a pretest. In addition I checked out the cold bloody water of the lake. High waves and fucking freezing. Little pussy I am: Swam only 500 meters. I couldn't even move my fingers. Yah yah when you train in 30 degrees water all the time and then open water swim with 14 degrees. Bad idea bro! So not excited about the swim for nearly 90 minutes in 2 weeks' time.

## Training on Solomon Islands

Directly on the next day after the wedding off to Solomon islands via stopover Brisbane. Next 2 days a mixture or sightseeing and training preparation for Challenge Wanaka. Accommodation a little tree house outside the capital close to the beach. Open water swim training could be possible. Yeah. Mighty waves made me thinking twice. At least no swim training at my beach house. My friendly host drove me around to cozy bays where is tested my wetsuit in 30 degrees water. Just checking if body could adapt. Swim in morning, run and manioc and fresh fish in afternoon. Yummi. And what about bike? The host gave me from his son a BMX one. 100 km sightseeing training on this little bike. The locals were taking photographs, laughed and waved at me when I passed them in the jungle. I guess they have never seen a white boy cycling on a kid's bike. I passed airplane wrecks from World War II, wild and not so wild pigs got chased by dogs, beautiful beaches and friendly people. 100 km bike ride. Facing problems with malaria since mosquito effected area. In a little shop I got the medicament Lariam. Took a pill and later I checked side effects: Dizziness, suicides by American soldiers. Hallejullah – On drugs for the next Iron distance. Yippi. If you don't have problems you create some. So I only took one, ignored the side effects and tried to relax.

**Short visit of Papua New Guinea**
Trip to Papua New Guinea got cut short. From 2 days to 1. Ok. PNG is also not the safest place anyways. So I wasn't sad at all. Travel training business as usual: 50 USD buy in local 5 Start Crown Plaza for 3 hours using the Gym. Split session bike run that makes fun. After that a nice massage in my cheap airport hotel. Oh lord. 50 soldiers were having a party. So marching army music took place and not Ayurveda relax ambience.

**Highlight: Cook Islands**
Another honeymoon trip ahead: Cook Islands. Politically still belonging to New Zealand but they count according to Wikipedia to the breakaway ones and have their own autonomy. Special when you fly to Rarotonga in Cook Islands you pass the date border. So actually you fly back in time. I guess nonsense knowledge. After a short night in middle class apartment on the main island off to a luxurious day trip to dream island Aitukui. Snorkeling, swimming, sun bathing, eating, easy drinking – major activities of that day. Good training day indeed. For mental relaxing short visit of a 5 Star VIP hotel with private pools, crystal clear water at lagoon. Couple of 1000 Dollars per night. Bam! Later we got a boots tour

with BBQ onboard. First time ever grilled bananas. Never had such a nice carbo load. On return traditional dinner show with yummi food and yummi dancing queens presenting local culture and songs. If you like you can also dance with them. They incorporate the audience in dancing and singing.

## Wanaka – Triathlon

At the end of the 2 weeks island hopping again back to Wanaka. Now the serious stuff of this trip to be ticked off. Challenge Wanaka together with Triathlon friend Jo. All the weekend festival and party for this race, suitable for the whole family. I was not looking forward to the swim having in mind my trial 2 weeks ago. But an Ironman has to do what an Ironman has to do – even when it's a challenge (triathlon). At least the beautiful landscape could be compensation enough.

## Lessons learnt: Dream islands in Pacific

1. When New Zealand then you need to go to Cook Islands. If Kiwi land is great. Cook Islands are even better. Honeymooners alert!
2. Another full distance Ironman you can find on the Norther Island in Taupo. Usually many more people join this race.
3. Challenge Wanaka is among the top 10 scenic triathlons in the world in different books and lists. It is a must!

# THE BEAUTY BUT THE BEAST OF WANAKA

When you read books about triathlon races that you have to finish once in your life there are races such as Challenge Roth in Germany for its great atmosphere and fast course. Or there is the dream destination of Hawaii for all those that are good enough to qualify to race at the World Championship. But then there are also smaller races with stunning landscape in combination with a challenging course such as the one at Wanaka on the South Island in New Zealand.

## Race Dream comes true

Since I started Triathlon in 2014 I always wanted to go there to take on the fight with the nature and myself. In February 2017 I did the long trip from Saudi Arabia to the Pacific to combine a wedding participation at the beginning of the trip followed by visiting some countries before the race (Papua New Guinea, Solomon Islands, and Cook Islands). Otherwise it would have been too expensive travelling such a long way. Disadvantage: Continuation of race preparation while travelling and using a rental bike on the race to travel more light.

## Preparation with Swim – Run focus

I seriously started just 6 weeks before travelling to New Zealand with the focus on Swim and Run since I believed the choppy 15 degrees water will kill me (as a bad Triathlon swimmer). I trusted my running strength would bring through the Trail Run with 300 m ascent by training regularly 50 km in the Trails in Riyadh. For the bike I just pulled out some 300 km weeks at mostly flat terrain or on a gym bike since the ascent was described as just 1000m. I strongly believed I could handle it with mental and physical strength to make a personal best by finishing in sub 12. Go big or go home.

## Just before the race – Shocking news

On Arrival at the wedding in New Zealand just 2 weeks before the race I met a Professional Triathlete that raced the course 6 times before and he predicted that it will take me around 3 hours longer than my personal best. In these days the temperature and the chilly heavy Kiwi winds would demand everything from the sportsmen and women. He gave the advice to get neoprene gloves and shoes and even a second neoprene cap. For the bike and running leg he recommended to have several layers that are wind and rain proof to stay warm and dry. "You have to eat more than ever, and you have to wear warmer than ever", he said. He made a bet for a beer that I will finish in 15 hours. He was so sure about it that I lost my confidence at all and I regretted that I didn't train more, harder, better. I felt like before my first ever Ironman: Unsecure, excited, and nervous.

## Sharing the pain is half the pain

Luckily I could join my feelings about the race together with former Riyadh Triathlete Joanna that prepared the last 4 months for her first long Ironman distance. Together with the support of a nutritionist and coach she was very well prepared but still excited about her first long distance adventure – especially for this tough one. Usually first timers go for flatter courses such as Ironman Austria, or UK, or Challenge Roth by chance. But her debut would be a real killer. Of course the reward for all upcoming pain would be the stunning landscape with lakes, mountains covered with snow, and green Italian style trees.

**Keep it small and simple**
The Challenge Wanaka festival saw around 2000 participants for the kid's races, the Half Iron Distance and the Full Distance. But for the full Ironman distance only 150ish people joined. That was a bit disappointing when waiting at the start line. No wonder: Ironman Taupo (on the northern Island was set up just 2 weeks later). Also the cheering audience alongside the course was quite small. Nevertheless they supported the triathletes with joy and happiness.

**Good weather conditions on race day**
For days Joanna and I were following the weather forecast. And we were really lucky. On race day morning there was nearly no wind and 9 Degrees Celsius Air temperature. That meant no waves in the freezing 15 degrees water. Neoprene wet suit was allowed – same as neoprene extra cap, hand gloves and shoes. We had only the extra cap on to minimize the heat loss. Imagine crystal clear, flat water surrounded by mountains where the peaks are covered by snow. Fabulous! Nevertheless

the cold water felt like thousands needles in your hands and feet. Surprisingly the swim went extremely well and I could pull out a personal best – side by side swimming with Joanna - per coincidence. Together we also mastered the T1 – Transition, put 2- 3 long sleeves on in expectation of the cold wind on the bike.

## Rollercoaster on bumpy roads

Everyone was happy being out of the cold wet and was seeking to get quickly warm on the bike ride. Aside of the layers when riding the bike it was also an obligation to have a thermal layer in special needs bag since the weather conditions in New Zealand can change very quickly. After a short while I realized the road conditions were not as great as they seemed by riding it by car. The surface was very bumpy. So the whole body shook up all the time. There were some peaks on the bike course but I felt ok. "Damn I should have made more hill training", I shouted when it came to even more hilly terrain. Nevertheless the track was similar to the profile of the so call Humps course in Riyadh. But the beauty of the lakes surrounded by green hills and snowy mountains covered up all bad thoughts. Joanna was in a great shape and lost only around 20 minutes against me on her TT Bike. Always having a smile on when I saw her at turning points. That was the indicator for me that she has still resources left on the run and her anxiety before the race were obsolete.

**Trail running as its best**

I felt great prepared for the run course since I made several sessions back in Riyadh on trail terrain, made best times on short races in Riyadh. So what might happen? Coming from the bike I directly felt it's not easy today. Legs felt not fresh as in my previous triathlons. But I started ok on the trail run with ups and downs but soft graveling surface – just like the material in the Riyadh DQ. Aid stations were around every 2 kilometers with banana, water, mineral drinks, and salty crackers. People were friendly and made a great job. Even I know when they shouted: "You look great" – I knew different being covered by salt and sweat.

**Up and downs with big surprise**

The first 7 km were pretty flat and I had a good pace. Personal best would be possible. But I got trouble with nutrition. Couldn't eat the carbo gels anymore and tried banana instead. But it felt not the same. In addition the terrain changed and the next 10 km were a permanent up and down, full of roots and big stones. The run was not easy anymore. But this part was close to a river with fabulous blue color. In all the pain I thought – that's the reason why I came here for. Great! I was so happy after this ups and downs. But the joy lasted only for 1000 Meter. After around 18 Kilometers there was a steep hill on a road. I thought: "Are you kidding me? That cannot be". I remembered the Dirab Bike training from the past with such challenging hills. It was such a great effort to run this hill. After I mastered this piece it was a pleasure running downhill to see the lake again and finishing the loop on the trail. In the finish area lots of people were cheering the triathletes.

## Beer will be waiting at finish line

Out of the blue the pro athlete that I made the beer bet with before the race called my name and was impressed by my performance. "I want that beer", I shouted to him happily since I knew I will win the bet and even believed I could have a great second loop. On my turn I saw Joanna just 30 minutes after me performing in a great way - still with a smile on her face. It was her day!

The second 21 kilometers where too much and I was disappointed by my favorite discipline. While having 2.10 hours on first loop I lost 10 more minutes on second loop. Due to the challenging terrain and not enough carbo intakes I finished the marathon only in 4.30. Not acceptable! Nevertheless on finish line I got the beer, the medal and a bit of sunshine at Lake Wanaka. In the moment on finish line I am always happy that the pain is over.

## Fast and furious

For future (not only Iron distance) races I need to check up the whole race details over and over to be better prepared – especially when trying to get hard and towards personal best times. In addition I strongly believe that before spending thousands of Dollars for a superb bike better spending couple of hundreds for a superb coach. That makes you faster, leaner and meaner on each race track. So I can start now for the next races in 2017. Highlight will be Double Ironman distance in June. Ambitious goal: Sub 24 hours. And apparently it looked like all set. Just one week after return to Riyadh: Marathon Personal best in 3.26. Even with a pipi stop. Plan was just to finish the race. Then turned out 4th place overall. Well, well. Recovery run it is.

**Lessons learnt from Challenge Wanaka**

1. If you love great landscape races Challenge Wanaka is your race.
2. If you love silence and no discussion about drafting on the bike go to Wanaka. Few people do the long distance. For more just wait 2 weeks and join Ironman Taupo on the northern island of New Zealand.
3. For Challenge Wanaka get prepared with extra layers of warmth's (2nd swim cap, hand gloves, booties, wind breaker) because it is one of the coldest and windiest triathlons in the circuit.

براكمان لـ اللمية : أرفع علم المملكة وفاء للود والتشجيع وهذه نصيحتي للمواهب

# بطل ألماني يشارك في سباقات كبرى رافعا العلم السعودي

أسامة البيكان - الرياض

البيانات الشخصية
الاسم: توماس براكمان
تاريخ الميلاد: ١٩٦٦/٢/٣
الجنسية: ألماني
الطول: ١٧٣ سم
الوزن: ٧١ كغم

1 Double Ironman report in Saudi newspaper

2 Marathon Kuwait just one week after Ironman Langkawi

3 Running in cold Antarctica

4 Bahamas – another dream destination to do a Marathon

5 Goose bumps when flying up the Solar Hill in Roth

6 Paid content: Angel 888 Real Estate in Thailand

7 Thanks to Ultra Specialist Matthias I could finish the 100 km of Biel

8 Swimming in freezing Antarctica secured by a guard

9 Robert Karas: World Record holder on Double & Triple Ironman

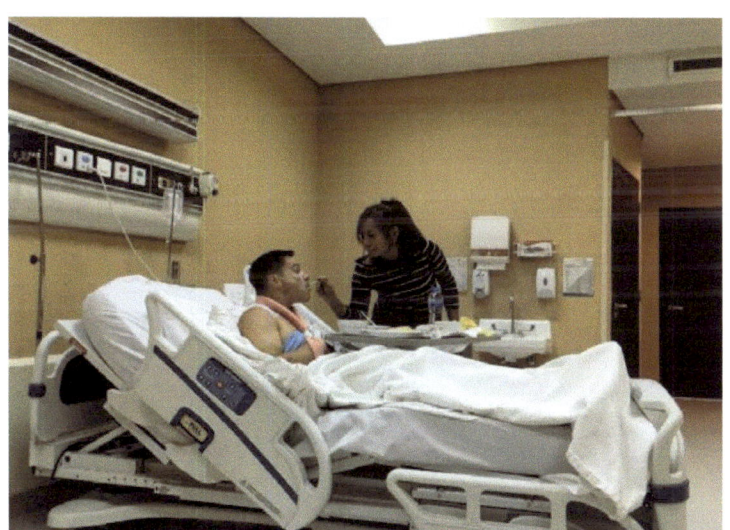
10 When you got a bike accident you get special treatment

Motivated Healthy Community

## G-FIT GYM Offering:

- Group Classes «Powered By LesMills»

- Personal Training

- Online Coaching

- EMS Training

 +966 54 103 6068
 team@gfitsa.com
 www.gfitsa.com

11 Paid content: G-Fit Gym in Riyadh, KSA

12 ITU Triathlon Abu Dhabi with fun loving Russian friend Sergey

13 Sharing the glory is double the glory: Beach finish with Jo in Mauritius

14 Morning jog in Buenos Aires

15 Winning a sea shell at the Bahamas Marathon

16 Paid content: Pacific Travel House in Munich, Germany

17 Ironman training in beautiful Seychelles

18 Dead Sea Ultra Marathon in Jordan

19 Beautiful landscape at the Challenge Wanaka

20 Dream location Mauritius to race the Indian Ocean Triathlon

21 Paid content: Excellence Magic Advertisement in Riyadh, KSA

22  Rural bathroom equipment in Togo

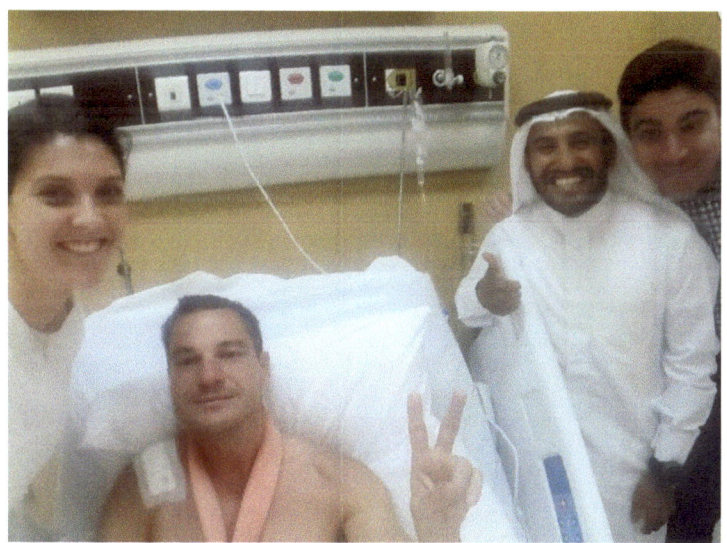

23  Friends are there in good and bad times

24 Family spirit at Double Ironman in Emsdetten

25 Upside down in spiritual Bhutan

biltongman@icloud.com    +27715725173

+966598936644

**We are a business based in Riyadh,**
**specialising in the production of South African style sausages & dried meat products.**
**Delivery & Overnight shipping available to all major centers in KSA.**
**Give us a call or send us a whatsapp for a quote!**

26 Paid content: Regardt's Taste of Africa in Riyadh, KSA

27  Flamingo formation on Aruba Island

28 Tough climbs at the Ironman Langkawi, Malaysia

29 Night run at the Double Ironman in Emsdetten, Germany

30 Together with Malta Triathlon Champion and Coach Fabio

31 Paid content: Angel 888 Real Estate in Pataya Beach, Thailand

32 Biking at the coasts of Australia

33 Core training with easy peasy equipment in Sierra Leone

34 Wolle - Top supporter and sub 10 hrs finisher at Roth

35 In paradise of Seychelles any pic is a good pic

36 Salute by Majed, Mo, and Sylvain when being in hospital

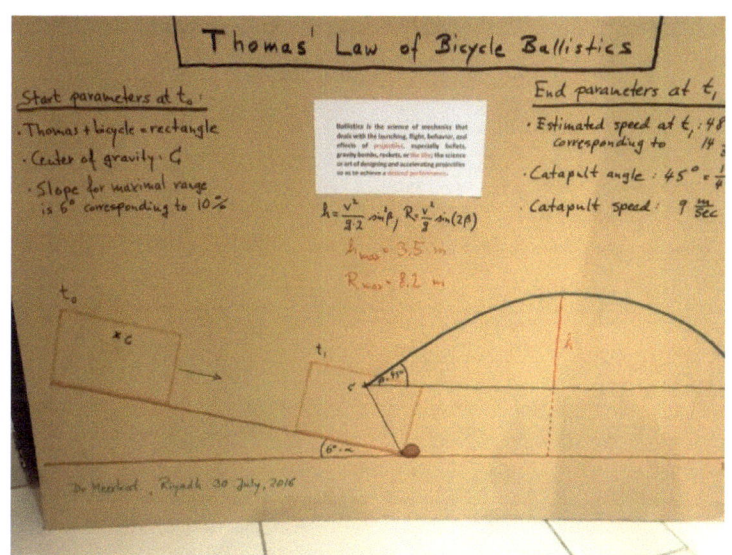

37 For some people triathlon is just physics – calculation for my accident

38  Paid content: Angel 888 Real Estate in Thailand

39 After a race is before a beer in a new country (Turkmenistan)

40 Sum up of another great travel and race year: 2018

**41 "Swedish Bumblebee" Kris finishes his Kona race in style**

**42 Salut to the post race beer on the red carpet of Challenge Wanaka**

43 First ever Ironman finish in Klagenfurth, Austria

44 Paid content: Angel 888 Real Estate in Thailand

45 Teaching Kids is good for stress releave and body-mind relaxation

46 Birthday party in Bucharest after Double Ironman & country hopping

47 Camel training in the desert of Saudi Arabia

48 Togo Swim at construction site

49 Who has the bigger eyes in Madagascar?

50 New Year's Eve party in Bahrain

51 Solomon Islands training

52 Together with Jo after person record at Ironman 70.3 Busselton

## PERSONAL AND PROFESSIONAL DEVELOPMENT

Feel that you could achieve more? Want to make more progress, but not sure how to go about it? Stuck in a bit of a rut? Lots of energy, but need a clearer idea of the right direction to take?

Have you ever considered coaching?

Introducing.....Mark McManus (Member of the Association for Coaching)

Mark qualified as a performance coach in 2009 when he completed the 'Open Executive Performance Coach Training' course in London. Since then, he has coached a number of colleagues, including high potential employees, and international private clients.

Using tried and tested coaching methods and tools, along with his own very relaxed and flexible style, Mark has successfully helped a wide range of people achieve their personal and professional goals. Coaching always focusses on moving forwards, on progression and attainment, and is most effective when it takes place in a positive, supportive and trusting coaching relationship. Sessions can be held via a wide variety of means, e.g. 'face to face', by telephone, by WhatsApp messaging, etc, and are always structured to review the progress achieved, identify and deal successfully with any obstacles that come up, and then prepare for the 'next steps'. A number of techniques are employed which will get you thinking in different and, often very refreshing, ways.

It is a simple fact that, the more effort and energy you are willing to put in as a coachee, the more you will get out of your coaching experience in the end. Coaching proves, time after time, that true teamwork really does pay dividends!

If you are interested in finding out more, please feel free to get in touch.

Mark

M: +44 (0)7534 055267
E: momanusm28@gmail.com

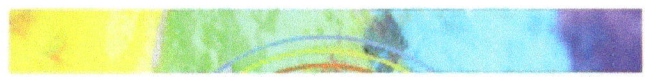

53 Paid content: Association for Coaching

# FORMULA 1 ACTION IN ABU DHABI

Before the Riyadh Triathlete season kicks off, the athletes test their form beginning of March each year in Abu Dhabi at the ITU Triathlon. This tradition is attracting more and more Riyadh participants, as well as good performances and even podium finishes. Also in 2018, our team of more than 20 participants saw 3 people in their age group and distance on the podium.

**New place – New Game – New timings**
In 2018 there were in fact more races: On Friday 3rd of March, the Sprint Triathlon and Kids races took place. While on Saturday, the Olympic Distance and the Maxi race went off. Aside from these new timings, the biggest adjustment came along with the new location: Yas Island. For the athletes, it was a better choice, since a lot of hotels were close to the Race Village including the start and finish area. So it was very convenient for the competitors for the pre – and after arrangements. Actually, most of the Riyadh people stayed in Radisson Blue after getting upgraded from Park Inn Hotel. So the comrades could align, and help each other before and after the race. For the first time, our club used the help of Sport Seasons Company, which transported some of the bikes over to Abu Dhabi. That made travel much easier.

**Speedy swim in Marina – Curvy Bike**
Together with the new location, there was also a new interesting course set-up. The swim was in the Yas

Marina with pretty calm waters. So it was very fast. Due to a current on the longer part, nearly everyone could get a great swim time. That brought some smiles onto the faces before heading to the bike leg.

## Formula 1 action
The highlight for the Triathletes was racing with the bike on the Formula 1 track. "It felt like the sports cars were flying around the laps", Henrik stated. He added: "But the course was full of curves and U-Turns. That made it more difficult, riding with a stiff TT Bike and demanded everything on the bike leg." In fact, it was a gear shifting festival. Only when you were able to fly around the curves and accelerate quickly straight after, could you have a great time.

The Run was a lap with a little hill, pretty flat though and shorter than expected. The predicted 10km or 20km for Maxi were short by a minimum of 1000 meters per lap. No one complained about it afterwards.

## Time for celebrations
After the races, the majority of the Riyadh Triathletes met in a Mexican Restaurant to have a good time, exchange results, dream about best times, and speak about future big races. For example, Kris Ahlin is on his serious way to qualify for the Ironman World Championships in Kona, Hawaii at the end of that year. Before, he will race the Ironman in Port Elizabeth (South Africa) in April and also the one in Kalmar (Sweden): Two chances, where he could qualify for Kona. Gareth Gallagher is heading to the famous Challenge Roth in

Germany in July, to his first Iron Distance. But, he is not going there just to finish. He wants to smash it – as he did in Abu Dhabi. On that night, Sergey, our Russian power man, got lucky and finished not only his Olympic Distance Race, but ended the night with a selfie and some small talk with the professional winner of the race and multiple world champion: Javier Gomez. Maybe he got some tips for the upcoming season?

## Ironman on a plane

Anyways, during that night, one triathlon buddy gave me a nice hint for combining racing and travelling and being more German like efficient: Ironman on a plane. Starting in Middle East and flying to Australia. Maybe 12 hours flight time should be enough to do that job. Apparently, in Doha airport in Quatar there is a 25 meter pool within the airport. A 3.86 km swim could be done. Then, flying with Quatar airways and booking business class and cycling on turbo and running on treadmill. That should also work. If you think this is too crazy? No! A British astronaut completed a full marathon in space in the last years. I like that idea, so I wrote an email to Red Bull, since a proper promotion and sponsor is needed. But the only response was, they are busy with other activities. It looks like I do need to be more famous to get their attention. Never mind, we had more beers and cheers that night and dreamed of flying - At least on the bike in the next races.

**Lessons Learned: Middle East for Racing and Sightseeing**

1. In the meantime, there are lots of races in the Middle East over the winter period: Dubai International Triathlon in November, Ironman 70.3 Bahrain in December, Ironman 70.3 Dubai in January, and the ITU Triathlon in March in Abu Dhabi. Best is to try one of these and combine it with a nice vacation, including desert feeling, camel rides, and shopping in the countless malls.

2. Starting 2019, Ironman 70.3 Oman is a new race. It will be held in Muscat beginning of March.

3. Abu Dhabi itself has got lots of attractions: Formula 1 Park, Louvre, and the big mosque.

# BEYOND THE IRON – DOUBLE ULTRA

When I asked an athlete about her motivation to run ultra-trails she said to me; if you cannot go faster, go further. So it will be longer but just with less intensity. Therefore I decided more than one year ago to apply for the Double Ultra Triathlon in Emsdetten, Germany. I believed I only needed to train the double distance but soon I recognized it's not that way and not that easy. Definitely it would be another level in triathlon.

**Training for the double trouble: Mental power**

Usually I try finishing a normal iron distance every 3-4 months of the year to have enough recovery time to prevent long term injuries. Plus still having fun for the training and enjoying other hobbies as well. 6 weeks training for an ironman finish of around 12 hours is ok, so I believed 2.5 months from middle of March to end of May would be enough for a double one. I quickly realized that I should have planned more time to be able to pull off extra-long training sessions.

If you step up to your next challenge its getting mental. You go out of your comfort zone. Therefore I wanted to trick my crazy mind by applying different tools:

1.  Positive race environment by swimming in a neoprene in a 50 meters pool. So no waves and calm waters. A flat running and bike course avoid the kick ass hills. Plus having three friends in my support team could boost morality.

2. Day long training sessions plus nutrition tests: When people complain about normal iron distance training and fitting into their social life including 40 hours work then they should train for double, triple or more. Up to 10 – 12 hours sessions at weekends took place. But knowing this stupid mileage in the body gave confidence.

3. "Train with the best to become the best". A nice quote by Saudi friend Majed. In fact true. Better athletes give you extra tips and tricks on the way even they never attempted a Double Ironman.

4. Relax time: Best are 2 to 3 Massages per week. When too expensive use a foam roller. Self-service works as well. Try to avoid stress people. Ok we cannot change out boss. But surround yourself with people that calm you down and comfort you. Try new things for relation: Yoga, meditation, or watching regularly relaxing movies or motivational ones. Find out what works best for you.

5. Keep focus: In a book I read: Ironman World champions are the most egoistic people on the world. And even you are a normal average finisher that counts the same.

**Hard, harder**

I planned to increase my training effort in order to have done at least once the distances of an 8000m swim, 360k bike and 84k run, however, I ended up doing

6000/295/60. In all these sessions I had breaks and split up sessions that made me worried for the race day. Nevertheless, I believed I would finish in around 28 hours (dreamed of below 24 hours) even although I only trained at 60 km run in a day maximum with having breaks. I believed on race day that I could compensate lack of training by swimming in a pool in neoprene, cycling and running on a flat course and having better nutrition and support by my team. So far so good but later in race other factors emerged that I didn't plan or predict.

## Planning is everything - logistics and team support

Several weeks in advance I had to order camping chairs, a pavilion tent, a table and an air bed for my support team. Due to overnight racing, there was no nutrition support by the race organization on swims and the bike leg so I needed people that I could trust to help me out. I didn't want to carry all the nutrition on the bike for example, so I convinced some of my friends to have a kind of "other camping weekend" with me at the race. Luckily, Wolfgang the head of my support team is a below 10 hrs ironman finisher and a rescue medic, so he knew specific needs of the race - physically and mentally. Also he gave me a kind of pressure not to be a lame duck walking the 84 km. Katalin, a triathlon beginner and good soul of the team came to the race to get inspired for her further triathlon career and was excited being part of the team. Andre the number 3 didn't have any bigger sports background and joined because we are good friends. I was happy having him onboard since in a weak moment you need someone telling you it's only swimming, biking, and running - nothing more. Later I figured out he was our social media manager for the race days and nearly half of the world knew when I was flying on the bike and having my downs on the run.

## Opening ceremony - meeting the world

I already got used to racing in an international environment having already competed in Abu Dhabi, Australia, New Zealand and Senegal, but here, in this little north German town of Emsdetten there was as well an international spirit. The athletes came from 17 different nationalities, the opening speeches were held in 3 different languages, the music group was a Scottish pipe band accompanied by American style cheer leaders. But one thing was different to other big races: It was the family spirit. Since it was a small race my team and I quickly managed to get to know lots of other athletes before, during and after the race. One that stood out from them all was Fabio from Malta, a triathlon coach with the passion for charity. Later our teams made a joint effort to support both of us with food, morality, cheers and massages.

## Race day - best weather conditions

They say: If you can think it! You can make it! So I tried to apply this rule but on race morning I was very doubtful - again because of the lack of training I had done. Then I remembered my niece who is suffering from blood cancer and I knew my pain will be over at least in 34 hours after cut off time, but hers is unpredictable. So I pulled myself together, took my team, the race gear and all the nutrition we prepared to the race track. Luckily the sun was up, no rain forecast for both days. Great!

## Swim - fastest among the slowest

It is better being a shark in a fish pond than a small fish in an ocean full of sharks. So I felt great when I realized that I was the fastest in my lane where people even used the breast- stroke. Every 1ooom I planned to drink, and every 2000m to take in a gel, but Wolfgang, my team leader gave me on a spoon smaller portions of the gel more frequently. So the time distance between carbo intakes wasn't that long. It helped me pulling off a great swim time in accordance to my standard: 2.41. He also told me at an early stage of the swim to avoid using my legs at all as the buoyancy of the neoprene would support. In fact due to this recommendation I was faster than before. ☺

## Bike - Pain at a descent level

Later I found out I was 32nd out of 67 after the swim. Terrific! I have never had a race where I was among the top 50% of the swimmers. Quickly I came into the cycling game but did the mistake of drinking too much every 5 kilometers as I did during training in the heat of Riyadh. Nearly every hour I needed to visit the toilet at the cost of 2 minutes each time, but even Wolfgang wanted me to drink more. However, I still believed that I would finish the bike leg in a maximum of 13 hours. After 180 km I had only lost 10 minutes to complete a 12 hours finish, but then I felt sick, no food intake was possible, I wanted to throw up. I couldn't see the carbo bars and gels anymore and changed to Haribo gummy bears, Nutella bread with salt, banana and in my massage break having pizzas. Other ultra-triathletes love to eat only ice-cream. Slowly the pace went down, and with extra breaks (massage, extra light set up for night) it had a cost on my planned timing. I tried to balance this out by riding longer parts on Time trial bars to save energy and to try being faster. I previously used this tactic for 70 percent of the track to avoid pain in back and neck. In curves and edges I was more upright. At the end I was slower but without pain.

But that one came later.

I finished the bike part in position 26. Until Andre told me, and showed the results on the big screen, I was not thinking about any position  All I wanted was to finish, but then I thought I could even move more forward in the rankings because running is my strongest part. I thought I could become top 20. Oh my god!


**Run - rollercoaster performance**

I was so happy being off the bike. Wolfgang took me under his arms and brought me to the changing tent. There I got quick but painful massage, new gels, bars, run gear and positive vibes by Katalin and Andre. I ran off like I had not done 360 kilometers on bike before, I couldn't believe it. It was close to midnight and my pace was great, no pain, on the score board I was in 25th position and I saw position 24 leading only by some seconds. That was a great motivation for me. Quickly I could go forward to 22nd position and close to 21. Then slowly the tiredness kicked in and I slowed down. In addition, I had to visit the toilet more often. At around km 35-38 I had my down, where I couldn't hold any intake for more than 3 kilometers. My support team got Coal tablets, Perenterol and Aspirin to fight my stomach issues. In this medical break I also received another massage, pasta, and motivational words from "you can do it" to "I don't want to be here until the afternoon". After this treatment I could restart running with a good pace again to around kilometer 60. Then from only 20 ish! Kilometers left to go it was torture! I tried to run but mostly I could only speed walk at best. At that time I hated myself for not having trained more. Or was it the stomach problems that caused the breakdown? Apparently the others in the race were suffering as well since I held onto the position of 25. Finally only 3 laps more, then 2, then the last. This one I tried to run again since Katalin and Wolfgang could join this lap of honor because each participant could hold up their home flag accompanied by their support team. I felt so overwhelmed that the race was nearly over. Then only 10 meters to finish line!

**Finish - The pain is over, happiness kicks in ☺**
After nearly 13 hours of running / walking I had finished. In total my time was only 29.32 hours. Only later on reflection after the race I didn't like my run time. But in this moment I was so happy to have completed it and to stop my pain. Only for a glimpse in time I realized I am a Double Ironman☺. In the end, it's just a race, only longer than normal. Then I realized the big hype people do for finishing a normal Ironman distance is questionable. Especially when I see that there were people in this race that had finished a Deca (10times) Ironman Distance. They did this double just as a warm up, even we do this next step in our achievements we should be always stay humble with both feet on the ground, but at the same time being proud.

**The heroes of the race**
Nevertheless, I was also impressed by the polish winner Robert. My team gave him the name "polish robot" because he didn't show any blink, didn't do any move too much. So he was very effective. Reward: finish in sub 20 hours in new world record time! One year later he even smashed the Triple Ironman world record in just 30 hours. But today here in Emsdetten there was also the Maltese record holder Fabio that has been training all life for triathlon. He organizes charity races in Malta and encourages me to go even further. But biggest respects to one Indian chap. We called him the Indian Dampflok. When you see him you might think he will never finish a marathon. Minimum 10-15 kilogram

overweight did the swim in breaststroke but finished in overall 33 hrs just before cut off. Later in the season he tried the triple. But he failed. But the remarkable result is after failing in triple he could finish the Quintuple Ultra style: Mind over matter indeed.

## Sum up - thumbs up

I will never forget this incredible race weekend. I had a great team supporting me and they helped me making it all the way. I liked the family feeling of the race organization and meeting all other competitors. The atmosphere was cozy and not so anonymous like in bike races with 2000 athletes. The combination of planning, training, flights, accommodation, team, and logistics made a great mix to me. And I guess it will not be the last double I do. Perhaps the triple is calling as well. Anything is possible!

## Race first, countries second, birthday party third

But that weekend was just the kick starter. I had planned 3 weeks' travelling with this great race at the beginning and a big birthday party in Bucharest at the end. In between: Ticking off several new countries on my list such as Niger, Burkina Faso, Cameroon, Equatorial Guinea, Sao Tome, Gabon, Mongolia, and Transnistria. Usually I stayed only one day in each place but with the still happy feeling after the Double Iron I could easily meet people. Ok: Beer connecting people. And in Africa there are a lot of different types. As an explorer I had to try one in each new country. However the final stop: Birthday celebration by club hopping with friends in

Bucharest including a stretch limousine ride including champagne, music and lots of fun. After all that stuff I did need vacation.

**Lessons learnt: More is merrier**

1. Overshooting is must for each leg: Best 8 km swim, 400 bike, 90 run / walk. It's good for the body and the mind because on race you have to do nearly all together
2. Test nutrition: Best preparation can be spoilt by wrong nutrition after 15 plus hours. Body needs more normal food and less carbo gels.
3. Training in race conditions: Night runs to train the fatigue and tiredness during dark hours
4. When team support: then the best one. Trust your people. In moments of sadness and pain they lift you up.

# THE MALTA MONSTER

"Hey man, let's have a beer, or two" – That were the words just before the Double Ironman by Fabio. He is the 2nd fastest Triathlete of Malta and is a triathlon coach for 25 years. Really? Did he really want to drink before the longest race he and me ever did? Thought we go to a tough event. But when I saw his ripped Six-pack when practicing swimming, I believed a beer in combination with hard long years long training should work. Ok. Beer first, then Double Ironman. But after the race I had to speak to him and we had a little interview.

**Former Pro Athletes smash the Age groups**
**Me:** You do triathlon for 25 years, but never qualified for Kona, Hawaii. Why not?
**Fabio:** I was always close but yet so far. My closest one was 9'35 in Sweden, Kalmar 2013 where I finished 8th in category and only first six qualified. The 6th one was 2mins before me. But as it goes along it is more and more difficult to qualify. In my age group (40 - 44) I am seeing a lot of ex pro athletes who are no longer good to challenge top pro positions but still good enough to win the age group. The second problem is these last 3 years the level has shot up, for example in Ironman Vichy recently there were four people under 9hrs in the AG 40 - 44

**If you cannot go faster you go further: Ultra Tri**

**Me:** Nevertheless you still have the speed. Now you go to 70.3 world championship. What's your expectation? What's your goal?

**Fabio:** I have prepared the best I could. Swim and bike I feel am in best shape with recent training sessions....running I had to decrease the load by 80% as had some calve issue. Unfortunately I have a lot of calve injuries when I do track speed sessions. That is also one of the reason am changing to Ultra. Longer the better and lower impact.

## Travel racing abroad

**Me:** Even racing in 70.3 now but you did already double Ironman Distance. Do you want to go even further? What is your motivation for it?

**Fabio:** I qualified for Chattanooga from last year, 5th in Ruegen (Germany) 2016 but I have always had in mind to do a Double Ironman Distance. I don't mind mixing distances as long as I have a good 3 month preparation. I have also won half ironman distance in Sicily 6 weeks before the double. My Motivation is always there. Never mind the race distance. I just love training and racing abroad.

## Long & slowly. Not sex. Stupid! Training of course!

**Me:** When training for further ultra: What is the difference in training in comparison to 70.3 or 140.6 aside of longer sessions?

**Fabio:** Ultra is another world. Most of the training is in zone 1 and 2. Long, long hours and mostly alone. But in my case it also meant fewer injuries. 70.3 require short, long intervals and quality sessions. In terms of hours for ultra you need 20 - 25 hrs of training a week in my opinion, whereas for 70.3, 15 - 18 hrs of training will do.

**The heart make bum – Falling in love with cycling**
**Me:** How do you keep your motivation for years? Have you ever tried different endurance sports?
**Fabio:** That's something I can't explain really. I think it has to be naturally gifted. Motivation is the key factor to train hard. I have been 22 years now in sports and I was never bored. Sometimes I am driving and see a few people cycling in a group at their training. Immediately my heart tells me how I wish I was cycling with them. It comes naturally.

**The finisher takes it all**
**Me:** What gives you motivation in a race when it is not working as planned?
**Fabio:** When things go wrong, like an injury or so, I do anything to at least finish the race and get that medal. I rather see a slow time instead of DNF.

In the meantime Fabio finished a Triple Ironman in Lensahn and cycled around Sicily Island (Italy) in just 3 days. "Bigger feasts than the Double", he said. Yeah, nice meals though!

# THE SWEDISH BUMBLEBEE

Kristoffer Ahlin is a very ambitious triathlete and a good training partner of mine. We both were racing and training together since I started in 2013. For years the married man and family dad was trying to qualify to Kona. Usually he was racing in Kalmar in his home country Sweden. 2014 he failed by 5 minutes. The year later he was totally sure and self-confident to do it but he had to give up after the swim. In 2016 he finished in 9.30 and failed by 20 minutes. Finally now he got his slot. I spoke to him just before heading to Kona.

## The winner takes it all

**Me:** How do you feel after qualification for Kona, the World Championship of Ironman Triathlon?

**Kris:** I feel great. I'm happy, pleased and thankful. It was a long journey on a "bumpy" road, but with a lot of fun and learning.

## Race with a smile

**Me:** What is your expectation?

**Kris:** I've been trying to work hard on mental development and always seen those "failures" as part of the road. It's like life but in a shorter perspective. You'll always find harder and easier parts. After each "failure" I think I also learned something. I have always analyzed them to try not to make the same mistake again if affect-able. The mental part hardest for me to overcome was to release the pressure on myself to reach my dream at the same time to keep the will to continue with the fighting spirit necessary to reach it. The Ironman slogan "race with a smile" was part of that solution. Run has been my strongest part but the lasts 3-4 years I've focused on cycling which become a favorite. I still like running in fresh weather. I now hope to experience that feeling in the water in the future.

## Making people better

**Me:** Always when training and racing with you, you see to be always happy. What is your secret?

**Kris:** Not sure what secret it might be. I tend to like meeting people and push and encourage them to do their best it they want to do that. Helping people is something I like which is also the reason for raising money for child cancer as well SOS children's Villages as part of my journey.

## Live, love, train

**Me:** How do you manage training time and having enough time for family and kids?

**Kris:** Planning and dedication is an important ingredient in the athlete's life. Of course it all gets much easier if you have a family with the same kind of interest.

## Balance of power and the myth of the bumblebee

**Me:** You are not as lean as other triathletes with your timings; you rather look like a weightlifter. What is your secret?

**Kris:** Ha ha...yea that's right. I probably would save some time reducing some weight on the run but the cost of losing weight would initially cost me some additional time on the bike as I probably would lose some strength. It's also part of my other life with might be the hardest part to change as changing the diet influences the people around me as well. But it is something I plan to put more efforts in. In fact a friend called me "the bumblebee" as they shouldn't be able to fly and in my case: I shouldn't be able to run as fast as I do. But honestly normally I lose some kilograms in the last 2 months before a big race.

# IN THE HEAT OF THE NIGHT OF LANGKAWI

There are many Triathlons with the label: "Race in paradise", such as the Ocean Triathlon in Mauritius, the Laguna Phuket Triathlon in Thailand, the Ironman of Aruba. In this category fits the Ironman Langkawi in Malaysia as well. So I decided to enjoy holiday feel with this Full Ironman in November 2017.

## 6 weeks build up for an Ironman – not 6 months

To balance out all my other hobbies I believed due to experience in training, and nutrition to pull out a good 4-6 weeks training before the race. Even having some backdrops with catching cold and other excuses would be enough to finish in an easy 12 hours ish time, of course always dreaming about personal best. Experience, mental strength and craziness would make it. In any case: Holiday race mode on for Ironman finish number 5.

## Bike back up plan when travelling

Unlike in Challenge Wanaka (January 2017) or Ironman Mallorca (September 2016) I planned to take my own bike with me even knowing it's a flight from Riyadh via Abu Dhabi and Kuala Lumpur – just for 3 days, longer weekend with 2 days extra paid leave. Since there is always room for failure with flying and having lack of trust to the airlines I ordered as backup a rental bike via phone before. In addition I took TT handlebars into my hand luggage. Just in case. Travelling only with hand luggage and bike case is fair enough. Most important equipment that I didn't want to buy or rent if luggage gets lost: Bike shoes, helmet, tri-suits, goggles and compression socks, charger for phone, race watch etc., all in hand luggage. Better safe than sorry.

## Forecast: Wash house

On arrival: Own bike didn't come through. Case got stuck in Abu Dhabi or Kuala Lumpur. I was unlucky like so many other triathletes from around the globe. Backup solution comes into play. Rental bike marsh, marsh! Planning is everything. Weather: 30 degrease Celsius with 90 percent humidity. Forecast for rain nearly every day. It will be a sweaty wet tough race I presumed. On the lucky happy side: Monkeys and friendly people all the way. On same day 70.3 and the full distance were conducted. Nevertheless the beauty of the hotel resorts and beaches gave push for upcoming race.

## Calm salty swim

Swim in open water. No wetsuit, 28 degrees Celsius in sea water. Bay protected swim course with Australian exit after 1.9 km. Swim was rolling start meaning people right next to you had a similar expected swim time. That makes it smoother and you can easier find your pace. In fact for me as an average swim performer it went well. Water was nice as it could be: Clear, warm, no waves. Great! Australian exit with 20 meters beach run in good time of around 40 minutes. The organizers provided drinking water on the short run part. Good stuff! I was happy since I was on the way to best time in swimming. Having a good start on that day! Even cramping up after around 2.5 km I bypassed others what indicated I am speeding up or they went slower. New PB after swim: 1.25. No wetsuit though. "Let's build up on that", I thought. But I knew: The day will be long and triathlons are not won by swimming. Running at the end will decide, like in so many other races.

**Monkey Bike leg**

Jump onto the bike. Plan: Every 5 km drinking, every 20 km gel, bar or banana. Plus every average 20 Kilometers taking the aid stations with extra isotonic drinks. Hot and humid conditions were harsh, very important to fuel with minerals and liquid in the right balance. Otherwise either pie stops or vomiting would follow, so far the plan. All went ok. I could keep a descent bike pace with above 30 kilometers an hour on the hilly rollercoaster course. Flying through little villages with the smiling faces of the Malay people, jungle like regions with monkeys next to the road watching the cyclists, and permanently changing scenery of rice fields and palm tree filled yellow beaches - Rushing through paradise.

**Too much rain over paradise**

Soon the clouds went dark darker and darker. Between 120 and 160 Kilometers it started raining. Cool. But as well dangerous: Now the little pot holes on the streets were covered and not easy to spot. Flying with 60 and more Kilometers down a hill with blended rain wet sun glasses: Not a good idea! Therefore: sun glasses off and praying while speeding downhill. The breaks for the carbo wheels didn't work properly. Fast and furious feelings came up. A crash would lead to hospital and extension of stay. Breathing was heavy, sight due to rain hard. I never saw people pushing their bikes up the hills. Maybe sign of weakness, but as well cleverness. Pushing the bike is sometimes faster plus energy saving and at the end as long you go forward that's the most important.

**All in on the bike**
In all my previous Ironman races I had to stop minimum once on the bike part for a pie stop, but on that day only once on the running later on. That showed me that all fluid I took in on that day the body needed desperately. However I slipped with my timings away from my best bike time I had booked before. Nevertheless, I pulled out my second fast bike split in all my 5 Ironmans. I was still in a happy mode. Last bit my strength the running part would come.

**Ice bucket challenge on the run**
I planned a running time below my personal best of 4 hours. But I could only beat the virtual pacemaker on my GPS watch on the first kilometer after the Transition 2 coming out of the big AC cooled building. Soon I realized I have to use every aid station for a little walk. Apparently it was every 2 kilometers. All the time taking

2 water bottles, 2 sponges and taking a handful iced water out of a big bucket. Cooling down the body was the key. Especially the thighs were in pain and needed cold water, and even cooling spray. The volunteers at each aid station had them ready for the athletes. My pace was more than 1 minute slower as I wanted to have. It was just the heat and the humidity that caused the slow pace. In moments like that I was wondering I could have survived the Double Ironman last summer and how I want to manager to do the Triple Iron distance in 2018.

But when I looked into the face of the other triathletes I quickly realized: When I am suffering the others do as well.


**Results: Bad but better**

When you go to an Ironman race you have different goals: Best time, just finish, or winning. But at the end its also enjoyment. Depending on race conditions (flat, hilly, wetsuit – non wetsuit, fresh vs. salt water, etc.) it has an impact on your time and performance. Even not having a best day – your competitors can have a worst day. And at the end you can end up with a very good result. If you suffer - theirs might do as well. So I finished with a slow run pace and a overall disappointing finish time. 30 minutes behind my average Ironman finishing times and 1 hour slower than personal best. But at the end I finished with best result in comparison to the triathletes in my age group. I became 48th place out of 200 starters. Maybe the others had to suffer more than me, the majority of Asians aren't that strong or I just approved overall? However: Positive take aways are a personal best on swim, 2nd best personal best on Bike and top 25% overall in Age Group as a good result and great memories of this beautiful weekend vacation race.

## Sum up and outlook

If you aim for a holiday and closure race season Ironman Langkawi is the place to go. It's not necessarily a course for getting a new personal best. But it looks like to have better chances to have higher rankings especially when you are used to the heat. Only some expats and triathletes from Europe take part. But these fellows had experience of more than 10 Ironman races in their career already. I had nice talks with such peeps about blood, sweat, and tears. Even when the Asian competitors qualify for Kona they might not go due lack of holidays, money or other reasons. The organizational team does a great job based on Malay hospitality, experience and Asian efficiency. Best is to spend around one week in the place to enjoy all the beauty of the nice island. Next Iron distance will come for certain. It looks like in 2018 aiming for Ironman South Africa in spring, Challenge Roth in July and / or Ironman Cozumel in November. But highlight will be the Triple Iron distance end of July. That sounds crazy. But after speaking to a guy having finished a DECA-Iron distance anything seems possible.

**Lessons learnt: Kona qualification via Asia**

1. Asian Ironman races look easier than in Europe since strong Age Groupers don't travel that far. And Asian athletes are not strong enough or don't want or cannot go to Hawaii. So better go to the role down the day after the race. Even with a rank of 40 you might be drawn.

2. Ironman Langkawi – long on the race market. Well organized with the smiling charme of the locals. And don't forget the monkeys as special supporters alongside the bike track.

3. It is good to plan one or two days in advance to arrive in Langkawi. Normally the bike case doesn't come through all stayovers on time. But hey spending more time in this paradise place isn't that bad idea.

# AFTER DOUBLE COMES THE TRIPLE

In parallel to the Malaysian Ironman race I believed that I could go even bigger. Since mental and environmental constraints hindered me for getting faster (hating swimming, outside cycling is bothered by dogs and cars, and running in desert is not fun at all) and longer: Double Ironman done. Next logical step: Triple!!! Easy peasy calculation: 6 weeks prep for normal Iron distance with estimated finish time of 12-13 hrs. 3 months prep for Double Iron. So Triple should work with 6 months or a bit more considering sickness, vacation, 50 Celsius heat in Saudi summer. Yo bro! If you can dream it, you can make it. Go big or go home! Rough plan aside of Power meter, heartrate monitoring, and each calorie counting: November: Every weekend another all-out race: Started with Ironman Langkawi in week 1, followed by Kuwait Marathon week 2, week 3: Ironman 70.3 Bahrain, week 4: Half Marathon Riyadh and 5km street race in Riyadh. If injury free and always full power al that could be nice and a good foundation for Triple Ironman in next summer with incredible 11.4 km Swim, 540 km on the bike and 126 km running at the end. Insane! But cut off is respectable 58 hours. So sleeping could be possible. But I dreamed of a finish in less than 2 days: 4 hours swim, 20 hours cycle and 22 hours run / walk. No sleep. No mercy!

## 4 tough Race weeks to get stamina

So it started: "Killing me softly" was a famous song in the nineties about love and passion. These days fitted as well into my life. In preparation for the Triple Ironman I aimed for the race to overload in training and giving it all without getting injured. Target: Always pulling out best time and not getting injured, and still be happy. Ok, before I forget: 40 hours working per week. What I would do as a professional triathlete? Racing every day?

## Kuwait: 1 day country

Ironman Langkawi was done. 3 massages in the following days, ice bath, Amino acid, protein dose and good carbs. Then back to work with sore legs but, happy mind. Just 4 days work then flight to Kuwait for Marathon. Kuwait – a classical 1 day country. Nothing much to see! I went there years ago. Before flying I asked a colleague if he had ever been to Kuwait before, and if he could recommend some spots to visit. The English man just said: "Yes dude, 1990 together with my military unit we fought for freedom down there". I didn't expect this answer. Nevertheless, he recommended the local national museum. Indeed that was the highlight of Kuwait City, the capital. The invasion by Iraqi forces was displayed in a professional and detailed style. It was impressive, with sound effects, smoke, and night lights. Bam! Bum! Bang! Other sightseeing spots: Kuwait Twin Towers, with a great view above the corniche while having a coffee. Another highlight close to the Hotel Radisson Blu: An old wooden sailing boat has been reconstructed and adjusted to host two spectacular restaurants. One was inside the belly of the boat. The other one was just underneath it, below the water line. In both they offered Arabic – Mediterranean food, and non–alcoholic beverages. Kuwait is also a dry country – no alcohol allowed like in Saudi Arabia.

## Kuwait Marathon

This time: Marathon. Legs ok. No collateral pain such as blisters, rashes, etc. The mood was ok. Just finish. No experiments, just easy pace. In starting area met a guy from century runners club. More than 100 Marathons down. Great stuff! Another life running goal could be achieved.

Surprisingly, the first kilometers went pretty fast, faster than I expected. Even with sore muscles, the body wanted to go fast. On the first half of the marathon the estimated finish time was 10 minutes faster than my personal best time. What is going on? Can I hold the pace? I could not! In fact I couldn't hold the pain and slowed down at the end. 3.37 hours instead of estimated 3.18 at around half time. But ok. Now relax and Ironman 70.3 next weekend.

## 70.3 Bahrain adventure

When based in Middle East there are some home races our Riyadh triathletes used to go to in their neighboring countries: ITU Abu Dhabi in spring season and Ironman 70.3 Bahrain. Super: You get for your 400 bucks entry fee: finisher jacket, base cap and a back pack. I guess the Sheikh of Bahrain gives some extra cash to boost the sport. But hey, isn't it a nice treat? And for the Age groupers a great deal. For European Athletes great opportunity to have a race in their off season and to burn some calories just before Xmas time is coming. Yo! Go for the Bahrain show! The Ironman 70.3 was just another middle distance triathlon finish with an average time at the end. Heavy winds killed the bike performance and the races before the run. Anyways: Another finisher medal in the box. Check!

## Half Marathon Riyadh 5 Km Charity race

In the following week back to back Half Marathon plus 5 km race. Bam. Missed personal best but won the 5 km race. Yes! It came like that: Sitting in office. I was a bit bored since it was my day off anyways. Ok in afternoon there is the 5km charity run. Ok. It's for fun. Then out of the blue I checked out the start time again. Hey, it's this morning. Hell! Luckily my car is always full of triathlon gear: Run shoes, pants, shirts, etc. It is a real sports car. In the following Charity Xmas challenge I was running every day 1 kilometer more. It was organized by the world record holder in backwards marathon running (3.40) OMG. Most of us are not even capable to do it forward. Bam!

## Triple Ironman Project full steam ahead

New Year: Still keeping it up to the Triple. Bahamas Marathon in January at beginning of the year. I dreamed about Boston qualifier, meaning 3.15 or fast. But after partying all night the week before due to men's weakness only 3.30 in Bahamas Coastal run.

Nevertheless I won a seashell as reward for 2$^{nd}$ place in Age group. What a surprise. Morality boost for the triple trouble to come. Then I was bouncing for 2 weeks between Haiti, Suriname, French Guyana, Cayman Islands, and Miami. Even an Ironman can be weak: Severe pain, sickness, and a cold after. Ok is all that travel and racing stuff really to hard? I had to skip different races. I tried my luck in another trial for Boston at Riyadh Marathon in February. That ended up in a disaster. So bad: The first half I was on the flying mode but it followed by being in crying mode. I still had some sickness still in the bones. At the start I felt great. But the weeks earlier had damaged my system too much. Bloody hell! That was not my day. But DNF (Did not finish) wasn't an option. I finished the marathon one hour slower than the one in Bahamas. But I finished. Lessons learnt: Recovery and sleep first, training and race second.

## Coach is not the best

Next steps: Getting a coach and pushing it to the limit. 2 Half Marathon races back to back in the next month. Day 1: top 3-podium. Day 2: 20 minutes slower but ok. Legs were still burning. I was happy and I knew it - so far so good. Triple Ironman full steam ahead. The coach was also happy. But he looked happy about anything I did. I realized more and more the professional Ironman coach might be good for speed training for normal Ironman distance but not for the ultra-considering as well he never did a distance beyond the Iron. But I wasn't strong enough to kick his ass. Stupid me! At the end I didn't do what he wanted but he did tell me what I wanted to do. I believed for Triple in ultra-long sessions. No real speed bullshit.

## North Korea Half Marathon

Visiting Saudi Arabia with closed shops at prayer times, separate dining areas for men and women in restaurants, until 2018 no cinemas and theaters is much more different than a trip to North Korea. Even sports events are a special case in Saudi. But both countries are relatively hard to travel to and to enter. The media image has a similar effect. Most people are afraid to go there. But hey more peeps get killed on the streets in USA than in places such as Saudi or North Korea.

## Marathon run

In spring 2018 flying over via a Tour Company to tick off this incredible place. In addition I am aiming for a full marathon. Could do lots of sightseeing, fast run people. The event was made for 5km, 10km, Half Marathon and full marathon. Tricky: Unclear toilet situation, bumpy roads, cold rainy, brrr. But every runner received high-5 by all people along the way. The aid stations were only equipped with water. Metro system showed modern transport capabilities, lots of souvenirs, batches and stamps, but only 3 TV channels. We got a city tour, war museum, could talk to locals, bars. Like in other communist countries wide spacey streets with monuments. Before the trip: Don'ts: No photograph, no leaving the group, no credit cards, no local money. But in fact all tidy, neat, and clean.

## Running with polar bears

Incredible runners were present: From beginners to Ironmen, multi marathon finishers, Boston qualifiers, Ultra runners. 2 of them made the Marathon challenge finishing a race on each continent including the Antarctica one plus the North Pole. Incredible! I want that stuff too: Running at − 30 degrees Celsius, having your sweat frozen to ice, breathing icy air and threat of polar bears. YES! Let's do it. The run is on a 4 km loop. The participants are protected by Russian soldiers with AK 47 gun. The polar bears can be up to 40 Kilometers per hour fast. So when you spot one and don't hit him with the gun you might have had your last moment in life. Observations though: Dog food first time in my life, no hand gloves by locals (poor people), propaganda souvenirs everywhere, friendly open minded people (even on Marathon high 5), Short skirts in cold (similar to Japan), and USA is the bad boy.

## The longest Day – 100 km of Biel

"If you cannot run faster, you run further", once a runner friend told me. After failing progressing on the Marathon distance and getting stuck at around 3.30ish it was time to step up. After 50 km at the Dead sea Marathon 2015 in Jordan and 84 Km Running part of Double Ironman 2017 now 100 Km of Biel one of the most famous and longest standing Ultra Marathons in the world. 2018 was the 60th anniversary for this spectacle. 100 Kilometers, 800 meters climb, thousands of Participants, Numbers tell the story. The legs tell the pain.

## About last night

Usually you see people posting things in social media how they got smashed in a party the night before with the hashtag #about last night. Here in Biel it could be similar. The party was set up: Stars in the night at 10pm, light rain, misty, 1000 party people ready to run, 80 percent humidity. It felt like in a washroom. Head lights on, vest to warm and legs in compressions – nearly everyone looked the same for the night race. All the peeps tried to master 10, 20, 42, 56, 72, or the full 100km.

## Rise and shine in the night

Bam! The start signal! Lucky me: At the beginning having the light of the street lamps I didn't need to put the headlight onto my head. Even it only weighs some grams; it's annoying when you don't use it on the daily basis. Later I could steal the light of others with bigger illumination. Running in a group made it easier as well. Nevertheless tried to slow down knowing 100 km could be really long. Strangely while I was running all the hills the people around me always walked them.

## Food strategy

I knew the killer will be in the night especially between 1 and 4 am in the morning. For this time slot I planned starting to drink coke from the aid station to get a little boost and to stay awake.

**Running Grandma smashed the Double Ironman**

Somewhere around 60 km, I got tremendous pain, pain, pain, muscle pain. I had to stop several times to loosen the muscles. Then I got passed by people: Even a white haired old lady got me. She had a shirt on: Running Grandma. Yo! That gave the rest to my pain, mentally and physically knocked. But as long you got pain you are still alive. Even it is hurting you can go on, you should go on, be happy having legs to move. Once my ultra-running friend Ronel told me about a guy 15 years old living all his life in hospital. No arms, no legs. He was wondering why she stopped running at all or why she lost the running spirit. He told her: "What is the problem? Why don't you run you have got legs? Look at me!" After she told me that story I never complained again. Since she met that boy she is running ultra-marathons on behalf of this poor little man being in hospital all his life. All this stuff having in mind plus thinking of the possible mistakes I did to end up here: Too fast at the beginning, lack of training. I guess I had a wrong food strategy. Who knows? But the mind was stronger, walking still possible. And at the end there is always the following rule: Sharing the pain is cutting the pain into half.

**100 kilometers for breakfast**

Luckily at km 70 I met the German Ultra runner Matthias. He usually runs more than five 100 Km races in a year. This one was just a slower one for him. Just for training. At the end he pulled me, motivated me, and gave me smiles. I was so happy having him there. I learnt: Even with limited training you can always finish. Question is just about the timing. Luckily I was far away from the cut off time. But, I definitely missed the 12 hrs mark that I set for my confidence to go to the Triple Ironman. However, I felt strong and happy about this next level achievement.

## Lessons learnt: Never stop believing in yourself

1. If you get a coach make sure he has higher achievements than yourself. Otherwise you will be teaching him. But a triathlon coach is cheaper than a psychotherapist.
2. North Korea is not the weirdest country in the world. It is one of the normal ones.
3. 100 Kilometer of Biel: That Ultra Marathon race should be on the race bucket list of endurance runners. It is a must have such as Wadi Rum Run in Jordan, Western States in USA, or the Ultra Trail in Cappadocia in Turkey.

# CHEERS AND TEARS AT CHALLENGE ROTH

Triathlon legends are made in Kona (Hawaii, USA) and in Roth (Germany). For Kona you need to be fast in races to qualify or winning in lottery after completing 12 Ironman branded races (so called Legacy program). For joining the Challenge Roth you only need to be quick for registration. If successful then the world's best atmospheric iron distance triathlon waits for you. 'Paradise' is not easy to reach.

## High end rental bike bam

So does apply for racing Challenge Roth. Even when successful to enter the race, the logistics around it are pretty intense. Roth is a little town with limited accommodation spaces. That forces the competitor to book hostel, Air BnB or Hotel up to 1 hour drive away from Swim start or Run finish. Oh yeah. It's a so called point to point race where start is different from finish location. Therefore I needed to book a rental car and a remote guest house. Since onward travelling applied another time another rental bike. This time I pre-ordered a TT Carbon bike with electric shifters. That cost me 400 USD. Oh man! But great service included for this high end bike plus company would pick up the bike from T2 after the race. That would save valuable time and effort to bring it back. Super!

## Blonde cheerleader boost

Day before race day I met per coincidence, in my little guest house a triathlon fanatic blonde girl crazy about this sport. The 20 something came only to Roth for cheering the other athletes – Age grouper or Kienle power pros. When she realized I am a starter she was all ears and wanted a ride to the start line in the morning. So I guessed she could be a triathlon groupie travelling around to all Iron races and supporting big and small players. But maybe she is just a fanatic cheerleader that soaks up the triathlon spirit to start her own racing career. Who knows? Well, I didn't believe she would appear 4 o'clock in the morning. The young bunnies these days would rather sleep long, I thought. But: surprise, surprise. Like a little rubber ball she was jumping up and down in the lobby, ready to ride: Short, shorter the skirt, and long, longer the legs. But as an Ironman I was fully focused on the race of course.

**Swim – Canale Grande**
Rolling Start in 5 minutes distance. A gun shot like in a war releases the waiting crowd into the 4.86 km in Donau-Main canal. High in the air: Big colorful balloons. It was a clear blue morning sky with light sunshine and 1000 of peeps cheering. Best race conditions ever. Moments like this you will never forget. The swim was pretty easy: 1.6 km in one direction, the canal down, turn, and all the way back and another turn around. Best is to swim close to the edge. There are fewer peeps plus it is faster. So I could pull out my 2nd best time even being lazy in training before. Good one: Every 100 meters or so there is a marker indicating the distance. Plus: You can directly look into the eyes of the people cheering for you.

## Bike – Magnificent Hill

Then off to the bike. I got rental TT Scott Plasma since onwards travel and no space and battle with a bike on the plane while travelling. First 30 km I actually had to figure out the electric shifters, the pain in the legs reflecting lack of hilly bike training, but soon all was ok in Ironman number 6. Two loops to do. 25 Celsius, sunshine, clear blue sky, lots of peeps at the course, little churches, villages all the way. And: Still ahead the famous solar hill. But it shouldn't be the steepest climb on that day. Greding- In this little town at 30 km longer hill but lots of cheering crowd. Bypassing uphill other riders while still in TT position - the Scott did its job :). The legs did theirs as well.

## Standing ride

Then: Rolling up and down. I was waiting for Solar Hill. Here it comes. The noise increased, the wide road went narrow n narrower, and lots of people jumped centimeters in front of you always and shouted your name. Making my path up the hill had flash backs of race legends in Tour de France like duels from Armstrong and Ullrich. That was a great feeling: Tears after the cheers. That made my flying on da bike. But crash, boom, bang at km 140. The saddle went down by 2-3 centimeters. And the sitting was only possible for short while. For me it was like: On the saddle, out of the saddle. That was the procedure for the last 90 minutes on the bike. Different muscle groups now in pain. Even a better bike split not possible anymore. All I thought: Hopefully the bike breaks not completely.

**Run – Flying and Chatting**

Then the run: First time ever knee pain. The age came to play? Or was it the saddle? Fucking, fuck! Should I first time ever to pull out of a race? At km 5 believed to walk or to give up concerning the pain. But as long the Cut off time was not reached and the pain was still ok to manage a pace of 6 min / km I would never ever giving up. Also a principle: If you give up once it can become a habit. The great Michael Air Jordan once said. So my conclusion: Slower the run lesser the pain. After the period of pain at the beginning, suddenly the adrenaline kicked in. Was it the cheering crowd, was the race spirit? Who knows? I was happy again. Up to kilometer 25 I felt great and asked myself: Is it going downhill now? I could pull out even a negative split on the marathon. With a new personal record on the bike already, I had lots of motivation in this moment. And really: Hoppla hop reaching km 10. The power was still in place. Even time and energy enough for a chat with a team relay athlete: Speaking about the nice sun, weather, the river that we were running alongside and the great atmosphere and support by the crowd Km 15, 16, 17 – tick, tick, tick. A new overall personal record seems in reach. Anything is possible today.

**Hit the wall**

Km 25: BAM! BOOM! BANG! Hit by a rocket. That rocket killed all energy. What was that? Out of the blue the pace went down. In parallel the gels didn't taste anymore, the stomach cramped up, vomiting could be an option. Slower and slower my pace went. OMG! I assumed, a very long day ahead. At least new personal best time on the bike I had under the belt. Kilometer 26: Nearly walking. Don't give up boy! Lord: Give me energy: Banana, Water, Cola, Gels, Salt? No. No. No. Even thinking of food and drinks was awful. The kilometers went longer and longer. 27. Lost on the next 10 kilometers nearly 1 hour by run walking, fighting forward. Just wanted to finish: Interesting how your mindset changes: From pushing toward a new personal best and beating yourself to the hardest to just finish this day. When people saw me walking they encouraged me: "Hey it's not far anymore. Run boy, run!" I answered: "Yeah, only 2 km left. It doesn't matter now if run or walk. Finish is finish." Yes: I am here to finish. And I will. As a takeaway: Another Iron distance under the belt. Ironman number 6 done. Nevertheless run at the sucked once again. Either needs more bike / run splits or better nutrition. But now I need a shower.

**At the end: Make history**
On the finish line: Surprise, surprise! The blonde honey bunny was waiting. I had forgotten her completely. Hug here, bussi there. Wolle Kuhl – triathlon buddy was waiting as well. He finished 2.5 hours earlier than me. 10 years younger, better talented, more disciplined in the hard training sessions. It is always good to have company on days of suffering. Sharing the pain is half the pain. To sum up this race: Roth – Magic is waiting. Take it. Get your personal best. Meet the greatest of this sport. And enjoy the hospitality of the crowd. 1200 m elevation gain on bike and 160 m on the run. Jan

Frodeno made here history with the world record in 7.35ish. Make yours too!

## Pulling out of Triple

3 weeks later: Original plan was to start and finish the Triple Ironman in Emsdetten in Germany. But after 100 Kilometer ultra-run from Biel in June I decided to pull out. I felt I am not ready yet. Wanted to test my performance in Biel where I finished in around 14 hours. 12 hours was my personal cut off for the Triple. If I cannot trust the running spirit of my legs then I should play it better safe than being sorry. In addition I had lots of travelling this year what caused lack of bike training. I felt I wanted it all: Finishing all the UN countries in this year and as well the Triple. So I switched to Ironman Hamburg instead. Since flights were booked I could use the 3 extra days to bounce between Riyadh, Stuttgart, Brussels, Berlin and Hamburg to get 4 visas for some African countries at beginning of August since I planned onwards travelling at the end of August.

## Visa bounce in Europe

Arrival Frankfurt, Train to Stuttgart holding a speech about Saudi Arabia at the local Lions Club. Next day 3 hours train to Brussels. Tick off Central African Republic Visa. Afternoon and Evening 10 hours train ride to Berlin incl. 3 hours delay and changing 3 times the train. Yes: In one day 3 more embassies to visit. In parallel: Calling different travel and visa agencies to get other Visas and bookings as well. Not the best preparation for Sundays Ironman race. But I believed I could manage. It will be just another normal Ironman. Another 12.30 hours performance since flat course and central European summer temperatures would apply: Every other Sunday racing an Ironman. However got a cold due to lack of relax time the days before the race and the bouncing between all the cities and extra hours on the German Bahn. But successful people never blame others. They check what they did do wrong. In this case: Underestimation of the travel impact onto the body and the mind. But at that point I didn't really care anymore: I got my necessary Visas for the upcoming trips. Countries first, Ironman second!

**Lowest sport point of the year**
At the race weekend I had no voice. 50/50 I can start. Got rental bike, registration Hamburg Ironman done. Race morning had pain when swallowing water. Under normal circumstances I would do just 5 kilometers easy training run but not a half day performance Ironman. Never mind: Triathlon suit on. Shoes on. Off to the race. NOT! In a glimpse of a second I decided not to go to the start line. Better not to race than race in shitty conditions and having a unhealthy knock on effect and damage heart and later my mind regretting the stupid behavior. Better not to start at all than having to pull out of the race. So I pulled out on race morning. 30 minutes before going to swim start. It was so bad, but also so good. No Stress anymore. Downside: Lost lots of money but I won or kept my health on the long term.

## Lessons learnt: Roth first, Hawaii second

1. Challenge Roth is hard to get entry slot and it is quite challenging to organize the logistics around the race (rental car, accommodation, point to point course) but the reward is the audience. The local population lives for this event. Unique!
2. Ironman Hamburg is new in the market but it looks very fast since the bike course is nowadays pretty flat.
3. Ironman Frankfurt is a good choice for onwards travelling since Frankfurt is hub for flying to nearly each place in the world.

# SPACE IS CALLING

Swedish traveler Markus Lundgren has lived at least more than six months in Switzerland, the United States of America, Guatemala, and the People's Republic of China, Nigeria and the Kingdom of Saudi Arabia. He did not start out with the ambition to visit every country, although he read about people who had with great interest, as well as about hard-to-reach countries and regions. Nevertheless he completed all 193 UN member states already some years ago. And he is still hungry for more.

## Better late than never
**Me:** What made you travelling all the UN Countries?

**Markus:** I started travelling quite late. My first trip abroad (not counting the Nordic countries) was with my family to Cyprus when I was 13 years old. I quickly started travelling more often after that, though, and when I was 15 I visited China with a group where I did not know anyone before departure, and by 19 I regularly made trips (on a shoestring budget) around Europe. First after having visited around 100 countries I realized that it would be possible to visit all of them and started planning on how to visit them all in clusters of countries.

## Safety first
**Me:** What is your advice for people who love to explore strange new places concerning budget and safety?

**Markus:** I have always travelled on a budget, which is possible in most of the world with the Pacific being the most obvious exception. Also Africa is expensive if travelling by air, but if going by land also Africa can be cheap, although for safety reasons not all regions of Africa are suitable for overland travel. As for safety, in my view, there is not a single country in its entirety that is off limits, but certainly parts of countries. To find out the latest information I try to get in touch with people living in the area and ask their advice, and only occasionally have I needed to hire bodyguards to be on the safe side, in addition to not stopping more than one night in the same place so as not to give potential kidnappers an easy target.

### Cash is king for travelling
**Me:** Spending a lot of money for all the trips: Was the cash well spent after all especially when you go to countries where no normal tourist would like to go?

**Markus:** I think the cash I have spent on trips has been well spent, although I have never tabulated how much I have spent on trips in total, although I know it is a considerable amount. I would rather die with lots of travel memories than lots of cash in my bank account. Many of my most interesting countries have been those that few normal tourists visit, e.g. Bhutan, Eritrea and North Korea.

### Travel the world and meet interesting people
**Me:** What did you learn after completing the entire world? Where did you have your moment of your travel life?

**Markus:** It honestly felt a bit empty after I visited my last country, Canada, in 2013. I had so enjoyed working towards the goal of visiting all countries that I did not know how to handle having reached that goal. I have learned that most countries with a poor reputation are much better than expected. Had I not travelled I would not have known, for example, that one of the most hospitable peoples in the world are the Iranians. I cannot remember having any real epiphanies during my travels, no watershed moments, but rather small revelations about how the world and people work, and coming from naïve Sweden, that the difference between what someone says and then later does sometime is quite big.

### Space is calling
**Me:** What is next for you? Are you trying to travel more to remote regions, in future going to space maybe?
**Markus:** I would love to go to space, although it will likely be a few more years until that is financially viable for me. I also have several regions left to visit in the world. Highest on my priority list at the moment is to visit Socotra, a Yemeni island outside of Somalia. I have two three-year-old twins, so since they were born I have been travelling much less, and mostly in the region for limited periods of time. Until they are older I will continue travelling only intermittently. Hopefully they will both enjoy travelling when they grow up; so that we can go together to places I have not yet visited. If not, I will have to wait until they are more independent before I can go on longer trips, e.g. by boat to Antarctica and the North Pole, to more of the inhabited islands in Oceania or to my remaining Nomadmania regions in Europe.

# TRAVEL MISSION ACCOMPLISHED

Timor Leste, Federated States of Micronesia, Tuvalu, and Palau – not every sun loving tourist has these four countries on his agenda. Much better known are; Bali, the Philippines, Fiji Islands, and the dream beaches of Australia. No problem: When you ~~get~~ have 3 weeks' free time you can easily combine known popular destinations with new places. And finally, the last country on my list: Timor Leste.

**Oktoberfest a la Australia**
First, off to Brisbane, Australia. A long weekend of parties, with a trail half marathon included. Relatively cool temperatures make the runners heart jump. With a 300 meter elevation the gain is a boost to your body temperature quickly. As a reward: Brisbane offers a few German related establishments, such as Munich Brauhaus, as well as the German Club, with an Octoberfest feeling, and big Beer glasses. Never to forget: Pork, Schnitzel, and Sausages. Eating, drinking and partying are great. Always better with great company. Therefore I had organized some nice peeps from previous and current travels to join me for this festive feast.

**Party crashing in Tuvalu**
Powered up by German delicatessens; off to Tuvalu. This little island country is located on an atoll. Theoretically, there is the chance to organize a swim

and run compilation to circle the island, since 5-6 times of the land mass is interrupted by a 500 to 1000 meters sea water gap. All spots in the tiny country are very close to the water of course, and to the airfield. Even the hotels are directly next to the runway. During the day people use the strip as a normal road. In the late evening people play soccer, or do their jogging. In Tuvalu, I met another English travel buddy that I knew from Saudi Arabia. Together we discovered this little island. Sandy beaches, palms, friendly people! Tops! And partying is always possible. During the check-in at the hotel I got along with a Chinese looking chap, Taiwanese: same-same, but different. In the evening there was a celebration of the Taiwan national day in the hotel. Great!. Self-invite for this festive event, but while having dinner and lots of drinks, a serious background story: By 2050 the country of Tuvalu might be vanished as the rise of the ocean waters would flood over the country. Solution: Save the planet save Tuvalu.

## Cloud 9 pleasures in Fiji

Ongoing to Fiji, Third time in my life to this great touristic well developed place. Fiji is used as a hub to fly to neighboring island countries. 2 days in the cozy smugglers cove hotel set up. This middle class hotel offers descent rooms with hostel parts for young Australian teens to honey couples from Europe. For each budget something is available. Always a good choice: Fiji beer! This year I planned a day trip to Cloud 9 – a swimming party lounge in the middle of the Pacific Ocean. It has all you need for a nice day in paradise:

Around 30 nice people, snorkeling equipment, pizza, soft and hard drinks, sunshine, crystal clear water, and a little breeze. Not to be forgotten; chilling house music. Definitely, it's also a superb place to celebrate birthdays, weddings, and other bigger events – in case you've got the money for this lovely honey.

**Under water love in Palau**
Snorkeling, swimming, kayaking, and sun bathing plus Japanese cuisine: These are the highlights for the little country Palau, in the Pacific. For a short period of time it belonged to the German Empire at the end of the 19$^{th}$ century. During World War I the Japanese took it over, followed by the USA. That's the reason why you can find a colorful mix of German and Japanese tourists. The Americans you can find anyways in the Pacific. Run training in the morning at 30 degrees Celsius and 80 percent humidity is heavy, especially when you don't get a finisher medal as a reward; only breakfast. However, the best moment was when an ex professional ultra-swimmer gave me swim lessons for improving my style in the water. She was a Tour guide through the world heritage sites of the island country. Splendid! After this little session, off to the German consul. Really? Yes! This office of the German foreign office is located in a little souvenir shop in downtown. But unluckily he was at the reception of a German cruise liner. However I enjoyed typical Japanese food instead for dinner in the little restaurant: Tora, Tora!

## Diving in Micronesia

3 days Palau, then Chuuk, Federated States of Micronesia. Normally you see here only dive lovers, especially those that are interested in wrecks. In World War II there were some battles between the Japanese and the USA. Japan has the most wrecked ships under water these days, enough said, guess who lost here. Lots of the Japanese ones you can find between the countless islands. Staying in Blue Lagoon Resort is a good choice: Handful of cats, some dogs as pets give you nice company between the dive trips that you can organize from the resort. For me, it's the best time to run around and swim in the great water. Dream sunsets are waiting; sun beds, chairs, hammocks, and lounge bar are pointed towards west. Palm trees, clear water, and beer from Hawaii make the sundowner perfect.

## Ugly eggs in Philippines

I had a one day layover in Manila, the capital city of the Philippines. Well organized by my travel buddy Ricky. By his guidance I could quickly realize in that one day: The people of the Philippines are very optimistic people. Nearly only 1 meter tall, they play basketball like crazy. Many of them cannot swim but live on one of the many islands. Sounds crazy to me!. On the other hand they seem very confident concerning cooking, and proudly present their dishes on social media.. Usually, for European eyes they don't look delicious at all. No wonder there are nearly no Pilipino restaurants in the world. Or have you ever been to one? Good, damn right. There are Italian, Chinese, Japanese, French restaurants even Irish pubs, and you can find German Beerhouses worldwide, but Pilipino style? No way! In addition to the infamous cooking, their major love for their dish BALUT says everything: It's a chicken egg, premature little chicken baby is inside it. They love it. Even writing these lines here make me nearly puke. Ok. Everyone has their own taste. But they are really positively famous for one thing, and one thing alone: Karaoke! They love to sing. So many Karaoke bars!. Germans need massive beers, cheers, and more beers to sing voluntary. But for the Pilipino friends: Easy peasy!. When their kids are born, they are not crying or screaming – they are singing.

**Been there, seen that, done that!**

And I am onboard an airplane again. This time it went to Timor Leste. Finally; the last country to go to, UN recognized of coz. Mission accomplished: Travelled to all 193 UN member states. Sometimes i stayed longer, sometimes shorter. People can argue about it. But for me: Seen that, travelled there, done that. Champagne wasn't available. So i took the local drinks for celebration: Huge coconuts! Then the usual stuff in the pacific: Beach house with sea view, Latino flair thanks to Portuguese speaking citizens, soft beach sand and again another splendid sunset in the evening, of course with a coconut. In the morning: The usual beach runs between 5 and 10 kilometers.

**Surfing in Bali**

Happy ending of three weeks travelling: Bali. Nothing can go wrong with this island. Ok. This time it was only a layover again. But years ago made it for one week: Superb massages, indulging food and riding on the waves in the ocean, a dream. For surfers Kuta beach is the hot spot. Same applies for lazy ones, and for sun lovers. For me: Sunrise and sunset beach runs, circling sun lovers in the afternoon, and yoga peeps in the morning. Overall: Great for having sundowners at one of the countless beach bars and restaurants to close a day and another great trip. Especially with happy hour drinks! Prost!

**Lessons learnt: Travel the world and race it**

1. If you travel to the pacific you can easily combine swimming and run sessions. So many beaches wait for you! If you are up to diving or snorkeling – here you go.
2. After heavy sporty sessions the Asian pacific stylish cuisine boosts you up.
3. If you are not in a positive vibe – the endless smile of Filipino's lifts you up

# THE WORLD IS NOT ENOUGH

Norwegian Gunnar Garfors is below 40 years old and travelled the world already second time. In 2018 he has finished another visit to all 193 UN member states. He is also not just a traveler to tick off places he also likes to tell stories about it. He successfully published already one travel book (198 – How I ran out of countries) and has another one in the pipeline.

## Conquer the world as early starter

**Me:** When did you start travelling and why?

**Gunnar:** I think it started when I was only 4 years old. I only had one brother at the time (I now have three brothers and three sisters), and he was 2. Our dad worked as a medical doctor on a cruise ship in the Pacific, while we lived with our mom in my home village Naustdal on the Norwegian West Coast. As we were too young to read, our dad recorded incredible tales from China, the Philippines, Japan, Canada and USA on audio cassette tapes which he sent us a few times a month. We always ran to the mailbox to check for the packages. The stories were amazing, and I promised myself that when I became an adult I would travel as much as my dad. I have now travelled much more than he did. With such a big family, before low-cost airlines, we couldn't afford to travel by plane, so our holidays were spent in Norway, Sweden and the UK (we took our minibus and caravan on the ferry there). I first travelled alone when I was 17, on Interrail around Europe.

## One time is no time

**Me:** Travelling all UN Countries is already a big achievement. What is the driver for a 2nd round?

**Gunnar:** I have been researching my book "Nowhere" about the world's 20 least-visited visited countries the last 18 months or so. Going back to those countries made me realize that no country deserves to be visited only once. I therefore decided to revisit every country out there, something which has also been good for comparison reasons with regards to my book writing.

## Western style kills the culture

**Me:** What did you learn from the second one? What was different?

**Gunnar:** Yet again I met people with incredible stories, saw jaw-dropping sites and sceneries and found myself left with countless unforgettable experiences. What perhaps made the strongest impression were the big changes from my first visits. Many countries have developed quite a bit, and more people have a higher standard of living – although this has unfortunately not happened to a large degree with regards to the world's poorest. Whereas it is a good thing that more people have more comfortable lives, the westernization makes all cultures more similar. That means that we may lose some cultural aspects.

## Get rid of stuff, get memories instead

**Me:** A lot of people love to travel but don't find the time or the money to do so? What is your recommendation for this obstacle?

**Gunnar:** A lot of people will never be able to afford to travel outside their country, and I realize that I am in a very fortunate situation, coming from a western country with a democracy, great infrastructure, freedom of speech and religion, high wages and a strong passport. Most people in the western world can however afford to travel by prioritizing differently and saving up. We acquire so much stuff that we don't really need. I prefer experiences, good times and shared memories with friends, family and people I meet on the road. No one can take my experiences away from me, and they teach me a lot about the world, different people and cultures, and me.

**Travel: Never stop exploring**
**Me:** What are your next travel goals?
**Gunnar:** To finalize my book "Nowhere". It is coming out in 2019, and I am now working with the publisher on the last details. I will for sure travel more, not to travel would be an insult to my mind and my curiosity, but I haven't decided on another travel goal or another world record attempt yet.

# REACHING FOR THE STARS

So: 30 minutes before entering the start line of Ironman Hamburg ended the Ultra distance season 2017. Ok. Country collection complete by spending hell of money, time, effort – Satisfaction, pride? Yes. But I worked hard to get the Triple Ironman done as well. It could have been possible. On the other hand: More people went to space than travelled to all countries. And I guess more people finished a Triple Ironman. Never mind. Always forward. Always I aim higher, always trying to learn from failures, downfalls, and getting up again and setting new goals. Since the universe expands: We as humans should do the same. We should reach out, go beyond.

**Forward ever, backwards never**
Next things on the bucket list in combination travelling and racing: Finishing an Ironman triathlon on each continent, same as a single Marathon, including Antarctica and the North Pole. Here I got inspired by 70 years old Brent Weigner who completed already more than 160 marathons or ultra runs in more than 160 countries. He aims for completing a marathon in each country. And that is not enough: He even run the North Pole marathon several times and holds several world records. Biggest lessons learnt from him: Age is immaterial if the mind is fit along with the body.

**Mind over matter**

So I pointed out of all my little experience some ideas I came across for keep fighting over my limited body to make anything possible:

1. Visualization
    a. Finish: Image of crossing the finish and reward afterwards (cheers from friends in social media and food and drinks)
    b. Competitors: In small races having usually the same athletes that you want to beat. Then imagine the Ironman battles between Frodo and Kienle, or at the Tour de France: Ullrich vs. Armstrong.
    c. Last piece of races: Usually the last parts or hill climbs think of easy jogs of training or hill climbs in favorite training environment.
    d. Overtaking spirit: When racing in tough competitions and I couldn't run the last kilometers anymore, and then I thought of a fellow triathlete with overweight and his happiness just to walk nearly all of half marathons or marathons. So believed when he can do it with a smile I can do same.
2. Train with the best to become the best
    a. If I train with better, more experienced triathletes I learn a lot about nutrition, being hard, mental strength, secrets to fit on the spot, or recovery. Before each

Ironman I am training or contacting one of my favorite club colleagues to get his positive spirt. He is my mascot for each Ironman race. Everyone should have mascot!

b. Training even with less experienced, slower people can help: Boost morality and being role model from them. By giving tips to others you realize your own strengths and weaknesses and to handle them.

3. Forced recovery
    a. Regular Massages, stretch sessions, massages help to clean body and mind. Shutting down completely
    b. Teaching Judo to kids helps me having another sport in mind but also calming down

4. Lessons learnt
    a. Writing down positive and negative things after important races / races with an impact. What went wrong, what went well. That helps for preparation for the next races
    b. Looking back in time: When results are not easily to pull off again I try to reflect successes of the past. What nutrition and training I did in the past. What circumstances were in place?

5. Trying new things

a. Equipment: From time to time it helps to get fresh motivation by upgrading the bike, the power meter, the turbo, new shoes etc. New fresh tools bring a bit more sunshine in the training routine

6. Balance your goals
   a. I am trying to be proud of my results in comparison with myself of the past (being fast, racing longer, being leaner) or even beating other competitors and winning a trophy. But always realizing that there is someone who is better and faster. Even when a race is not going as planned there is something to build on and having a positive take away. For example having a bad Ironman time it is not the end of the world when your result in the completion is one of the best.

**Next goals**

With a strong mind and an average body great things can be possible. There are still so many nice races, challenges, and adventures out there: Marathon des Sables, Quintuple Ironman (5 Ironman on 5 days), the Ultra man series, Quadrathlon sport (Triathlon plus Kayak). Never to be forgotten: Kona (Ironman World Championship) and Boston (Marathon). For both speed work is necessary. And: much more to come: 7 summits, space travelling, Moon, Mars? There are so many temptations.